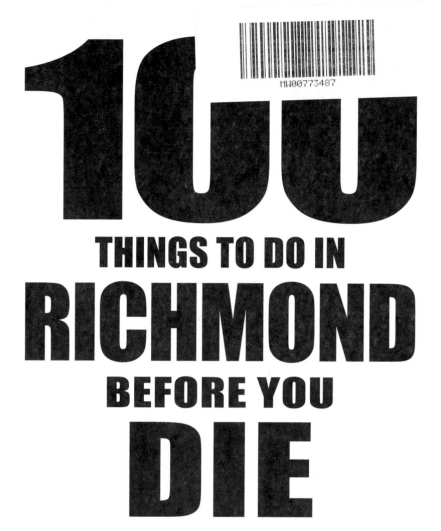

100

THINGS TO DO IN

RICHMOND

BEFORE YOU

DIE

MW00773487

Richmond skyline during Friday Cheers
Credit: Dave Parrish Photography

100
THINGS TO DO IN
RICHMOND
BEFORE YOU
DIE

• •

ANNIE TOBEY

REEDY PRESS

Copyright © 2023 by Reedy Press, LLC
Reedy Press
PO Box 5131
St. Louis, MO 63139, USA
www.reedypress.com

No part of this publication may be reproduced or transmitted in any form or by any means, electronic or mechanical, including photocopy, recording, or any information storage and retrieval system, without permission in writing from the publisher.

Permissions may be sought directly from Reedy Press at the above mailing address or via our website at www.reedypress.com.

Library of Congress Control Number: 2023938762

ISBN: 9781681064703

Design by Jill Halpin

All photos are by the author unless otherwise noted.

Printed in the United States of America
23 24 25 26 27   5 4 3 2 1

We (the publisher and the author) have done our best to provide the most accurate information available when this book was completed. However, we make no warranty, guarantee, or promise about the accuracy, completeness, or currency of the information provided, and we expressly disclaim all warranties, express or implied. Please note that attractions, company names, addresses, websites, and phone numbers are subject to change or closure, and this is outside of our control. We are not responsible for any loss, damage, injury, or inconvenience that may occur due to the use of this book. When exploring new destinations, please do your homework before you go. You are responsible for your own safety and health when using this book.

DEDICATION

With all my love to Daniel, Brian, and Rachel,
who gave me the three best reasons to stay in Richmond and
experience all that our city has to offer.

The Answer Brewpub
Credit: Tricia Anderson/Virginia Tourism Corporation

CONTENTS

Preface xiv

Acknowledgments xvi

Food and Drink

1. See Why It's All Greek to Us at Stella's 2

2. Get Boxed In with a Smile at Sally Bell's Kitchen 3

3. Elevate Your Dining at L'Opossum 4

4. Worship High Cuisine on Church Hill 5

5. Get a Taste of Richmond's History at Ukrop's Market Hall 6

6. Spoil Your Sweet Tooth at Shyndigz 8

7. Go Whole Hog at La Milpa 9

8. Dine in History at the Jefferson 10

9. Take Your Taste Buds to the Tropics at Carena's 12

10. Get a Taste of Cuban Cuisine at Kuba Kuba 13

11. Find the Answer to RVA Beer and Vietnamese Fare at Mekong and The Answer 14

12. Follow the Richmond Beer Trail 15

13. Don't Worry, Be Hoppy with Hazy Richmond IPAs 16

14. See What the Buzz Is About with Mead and Cider 18

15. Get in the Spirit with Craft Distilleries 20

• •

16. Roll Up Your Sleeves at a Cooking Class **22**

17. Wine Down on the Banks of the James at Upper Shirley Vineyards **23**

18. Savor a Perfect Pairing **24**

19. Appreciate the Evolution of BBQ at ZZQ **25**

20. Find Your Cheers at The Jasper **26**

21. Try the Threesome of Beer, Burgers, and Adult Shakes at Station 2 ...... **27**

22. Get Twisted at GWARbar **28**

23. Conjure a Beloved Italian Grandmother at Edo's Squid **29**

24. Catch the Soul of the City **30**

Music and Entertainment

25. Catch a Classic at the Classic Byrd Theatre **34**

26. See Why Richmond Is a Happening Place for Music
at The National **35**

27. Laugh until You Cry at Local Comedy Venues **36**

28. Have a One-Stop Night Out at The Tin Pan **38**

29. Get Creative at the Visual Arts Center of Richmond **39**

30. Surround Yourself with World Culture at the Richmond
Folk Festival **40**

31. Get Swept Up in the Drama at a Local Theater **42**

32. Be Entertained at Ornate Historic Venues **44**

33. Learn through Fun at the Children's Museum of Richmond **45**

34. Have a Wild, Aww-Mazing Time at the Metro Richmond Zoo **46**

• •

35. Eat, Drink, and Be Merry All under One Roof **48**

36. Catch a Performance at Firehouse Theatre **50**

37. Dance like You're in the Tropics at Havana '59 .... **51**

38. Get in the Christmas Spirit with Richmond's Holiday Lights **52**

39. Celebrate Fabulous Diversity at Godfrey's Drag Brunch..................... **53**

40. Putter Away Your Time at Hotel Greene **54**

41. Party at Richmond's Longest-Running Concert Series,
Friday Cheers **55**

42. Fill Your Mind with Arts at UR and VCU **56**

43. Let the Music String You Along with the Richmond Symphony **57**

Sports and Recreation

44. Traverse the Trails of the James River Park System............................. **60**

45. "Have Funn and Go Nuts" with the Flying Squirrels **61**

46. Find a Park Lover's Paradise at Pocahontas State Park........................ **62**

47. Get a Kick Out of the Richmond Kickers **63**

48. Cruise the Virginia Capital Trail **64**

49. Traverse Four Unique Trails along the James **66**

50. Chill Out, Work Out, or Rock Out at Dominion Riverrock **68**

51. Rev Up Your Engines at Richmond Raceway **69**

52. Run with a Gang . . . of Runners with Sports Backers and RRRC **70**

53. Go Fish on the James **71**

54. Go Mountain Biking on the Region's Trails with Riverside Cycling ... **72**

• •

55. Get Carried Away on the James River with Riverside Outfitters.......... **73**

56. Climb the Wall at the Old Manchester Bridge **74**

57. Take a Child to Play and Learn to Love at PARK365........................... **75**

58. Be Part of a 2,000-Year-Old Tradition at the Richmond International
Dragon Boat Festival.. **76**

59. Treat Your Dog to a Romp at Ruff Canine Club **77**

60. Have a Fun Fling with Disc Golf at Gillie's Creek Park **78**

Culture and History

61. Immerse Yourself in Richmond's History with the Valentine **82**

62. Engage with History at the Virginia Museum of History & Culture.... **83**

63. Marvel at Worldwide Creativity, Thoughtfulness, and Beauty
at the VMFA... **84**

64. Explore a Bounty of Flowers and Fun at Lewis Ginter
Botanical Garden.. **85**

65. Visit Plants, Animals, and the Gilded Age at Maymont **86**

66. Raise a Toast to UnHappy Hour at the Poe Museum........................... **87**

67. Be Inspired at the Maggie L. Walker House **88**

68. Celebrate Resilience and Brilliance in Jackson Ward **89**

69. Mourn Historic Injustice and Agony on the Richmond Slave Trail...... **90**

70. Contemplate Sobering Truths at the Virginia Holocaust Museum....... **91**

71. Get a Capital Perspective on Civil War History **92**

72. Discover Liberty in Church Hill and Historic St. John's Church.......... **94**

73. Get Spooky with Haunts of Richmond.. **96**

74. Celebrate the Life of a Richmond GOAT
at the Arthur Ashe Monument.. **97**

75. Salute the Dead and the Views at Hollywood Cemetery **98**

76. See How Art Beautifies and Inspires with Richmond's Murals........... **100**

77. Travel 400 Years Back in Time at Henricus Historical Park................ **102**

78. Have a Ball with STEM at the Science Museum of Virginia............... **103**

79. Pay Your Respects at the Virginia War Memorial............................... **104**

80. Get Artsy with First Friday Art Walks **105**

81. Get Derailed at the Richmond Railroad Museum **106**

82. See Where Wheels of Power Turn at the Virginia State Capitol
and Capitol Square **107**

Shopping and Fashion

83. Shop the Mile of Style in Carytown **110**

84. Feast and Fest on Virginia Fresh at the RVA Big Market **112**

85. Give a Gift of Richmond at the Valentine Museum Shop.................... **114**

86. Outfit Your Body and Soul at AlterNatives Boutique **115**

87. Get a Tattoo in RVA **116**

88. Shop the Past for Classic Styles at Bygones Vintage **118**

89. Find Down-Home Friendly alongside Global Influences
at Shakoor's Merchandise... **119**

90. Bring Your Perfect Art Home from Crossroads Art Center................. **120**

• •

91. Delight in Diverse Shopping at The Shops at 5807 ....**121**

92. Start Your Tropical Orchid Collection at Chadwick & Son Orchids....**122**

93. "Meat" Your Next Great Home-Cooked Meal at Belmont Butchery ...**124**

94. Find Your Groove at Plan 9 Music **125**

95. Be Dogged in Your Search for Curious Gifts at Mongrel....................**126**

96. Bring Your Home into the Modern World at LaDiff.............................**127**

97. Find New Old Décor at Caravati's Architectural Salvage **128**

98. Catch Good Vibes at Alchemists **129**

99. Train Your Sights on Small-Town Charm in Ashland **130**

100. Turn Over a New Leaf at Independent Bookstores **132**

Activities by Season **134**
Suggested Itineraries **136**
Index **139**

The Town of Ashland
Credit: Sarah Ann Atkins/Virginia Tourism Corporation

PREFACE

The Richmond region is steeped in history, yet it marches steadfastly into a brighter future. The city's location on the fall line of the James River has shaped its story while providing abundant beauty and natural recreation. The river and the people are bursting with vision and new ideas, nurturing the opportunities for world-class restaurants, craft beverages, arts, history, shopping, and entertainment.

Several Indigenous tribes made their home in this region, including the Powhatan, Chickahominy, Youghtanund, and Arrohateck. Some of the continent's earliest European settlers arrived here in the 17th century, soon after setting foot in the New World. They eventually settled in Richmond, displacing the natives. The young settlement had a hand in the American Revolution and hosted numerous Founding Fathers, including George Washington, Thomas Jefferson, and Patrick Henry. Many people know Richmond primarily as the capital of the Confederacy, but the city is tackling a more complete reckoning of its history, the virtue and the vice.

Today, public art and museums explore Richmond's history and progress. Our reputation has grown for things we can be unabashedly proud of: craft beer, independent restaurants, outdoor recreation, tattoos, and more. We've adopted a new moniker, too: RVA.

• •

The region's growing success caused my greatest challenge in crafting this book: "100 Things" merely scratches the surface! While new worthwhile places are popping up weekly, I focused primarily on those that have stood the test of time, becoming classics in their own right. It pained me to leave some out, so I beg apologies of Richmond locals whose favorites aren't included. Hopefully, though, long-time Richmonders and visitors will find new favorite places to enjoy and cherish.

Whether you're a local, a visitor, or just looking to learn, you can explore at least 100 things that make the Richmond region a place of beauty, fun, adventure, laughter, learning, and love.

ACKNOWLEDGMENTS

A host of friends, including coworkers and a multitude of Facebook friends, helped me out by sharing their local favorites. To all, I give my most sincere appreciation. My gratitude goes especially to those who helped with my "research": Ronda Ford, Brian Marsh, Rachel Marsh, Carena Ives, Paula Inserra, Marit Bank, and Tommie Klise.

Many thanks to John Bryan, author of *The James River in Richmond*, for his advice on fishing the James River and his other river tips; to Max Pendergraph and Phaedra Hise for their patience during mountain biking lessons at Pocahontas State Park; to Jenni Kirby of Crossroads Art Center for her guidance on Richmond art; to Maria Gallegos for her shopping tips; to Andrew Cothern, author of *RVA Playlist*, for his musical insights; and to Richmond's craft beer and running communities, who have given me more reasons to love the people and places of RVA.

Thanks to the many professionals who helped me better appreciate their organizations: Jennifer Guild at the Science Museum of Virginia, Haley McLaren at the Valentine Museum, Melissa Abernathy at Maymont, Taylor Fuqua of the Virginia Museum of History and Culture, Sarah Moseley at the Children's Museum of Richmond, Liz Nance of Virginia Repertory Theatre, Morgan Floyd at Henricus Historical Park, Erika Gay of Venture Richmond, Ben Terry of Richmond Flying Squirrels, Chris

• •

Houlihan at Haunts of Richmond, Beth Monroe of Lewis Ginter Botanical Garden, Clarissa Bannor at the Visual Arts Center of Richmond, Taylor Andelin at the Metro Richmond Zoo, and the staff at Richmond Region Tourism. And to the tour guides, servers, and others who shared with me their love for their businesses and organizations.

Thanks to Reedy Press for giving me the opportunity to share my love for my hometown.

And much gratitude to my four-legged buddy, Newt, who explored the dog-friendly venues with me, entirely without complaint.

Alewife
Credit: Lee Gregory/Virginia Tourism Corporation

FOOD
AND DRINK

SEE WHY
IT'S ALL GREEK TO US AT STELLA'S

Two waves of immigration brought entrepreneurial Greeks and their culture to Richmond's melting pot. Greek restaurants and an annual festival have affirmed locals' appreciation for that culture, especially the food. The Greek Festival, held at Saints Constantine and Helen Greek Orthodox Cathedral, began in 1976 and presents food, dancing, cathedral tours, a market, and opportunities to learn about the Greek culture and Eastern Orthodox religion. Several Richmond restaurants offer access to Mediterranean fare year-round. The most notable, Stella's, opened in 1983 and is named for matriarch and chef Stella Kafantaris Dikos. Stella's restaurant and its gourmet market offshoots use fresh ingredients and Greek authenticity to bring the best of the Old World to Richmond. Think pastichio, moussaka, spanakopita, souvlaki, tabouli, and flaming saganaki cheese. Opa!

Stella's
1012 Lafayette St., 804-358-2011
stellasrichmond.com

Richmond Greek Festival
Saints Constantine and Helen Greek
Orthodox Cathedral, 30 Malvern Ave.
greekfestival.com

TIP
Be early or be prepared to wait at Stella's and the festival. You can get prepackaged Greek foods at Stella's markets (see stellasrichmond.com for locations), though fresh is always better. Don't miss Stella Dikos's favorite, the spanakopita.

GET BOXED IN WITH A SMILE
AT SALLY BELL'S KITCHEN

Box lunches are traditions at this family-owned lunch spot that's been serving Richmonders since 1926. To-go boxes are lined with checkerboard paper, filled with a sandwich, a side of potato salad or macaroni salad, deviled egg half, cheese wafer topped with a pecan, and a cupcake. Embrace tradition and request twine rather than tape to secure your box. Classic Southern foods secure Sally Bell's place in Richmond culinary traditions. Items include egg salad, chicken salad, pimento cheese spread, and Smithfield ham sandwiches as well as legendary potato salad, and lemon chess, sweet potato, and pecan pies and tarts. You'll swear someone's Southern grandma made them. The cupcakes, however, stand out icing covers each cake on the top and on the sides. Makes one wonder why all cupcakes aren't iced like Sally Bell's!

2337 W Broad St., 804-644-2838
sallybellskitchen.com

ELEVATE YOUR DINING
AT L'OPOSSUM

The name offers your first clue to the creativity at L'Opossum sur la Colline de l'Orégon. It blends sensibilities of France and the American South and sprinkles in a dash of humor. The décor at this debaucherous playground for sophisticates provides the next hint: irreverent and eccentric art, like whimsical opossums, miniatures of Michelangelo's *David*, and *Star Wars* collectibles. The atmosphere is enhanced by a one-of-a-kind music playlist. The menu scintillates the funny bone and the appetite: like the "French Tickler" cocktail, oysters "in a green fairy fog of absinthe mist" and "braised pork belly à la Leviticus, a sinful temptation too good to Passover." But it's the food that ties the experience in one hugely delicious bow. From appetizer to dessert, each dish pulls together inspired ingredient combinations that play on the palate like a masterful Samuel Barber opera. Award-winning L'Opossum provides a feast for all senses.

626 China St., 804-918 6028
lopossum.com

WORSHIP HIGH CUISINE
ON CHURCH HILL

This historic neighborhood offers an astonishing concentration of culinary businesses nestled in a neighborhood of 19th-century homes. Patrick Henry's Pub & Grille and Liberty Public House embrace Church Hill's "Give me liberty or give me death" spirit. Fine-dining restaurants elevate eating out: The Roosevelt gives an upscale twist to Southern cuisine; Metzger Bar & Butchery harbors an affinity for German fare and meats; Alewife highlights Virginia coastal seafood; and Grisette boasts Old-World European cuisine. Looking for casual? Go for simply delicious at Cobra Burger; comfort food at The Hill Café; distinctively delicious ice cream at Spotty Dog; hand-milled, wood-fired breads and baked goods at Sub Rosa; authentic, friendly Ethiopian at The Nile; and savory and sweet New Zealand–style pies to go at Proper Pie. Make reservations and place takeout orders far ahead, because these popular establishments fill up and their items sell out.

The Roosevelt
623 N 25th St., 804-658-1935
rooseveltrva.com

Proper Pie
2505 E Broad St., #100, 804-343-7437
properpieco.com

Alewife
3120 E Marshall St., 804-325-3426
alewiferva.com

Spotty Dog Ice Cream Co.
2416 Jefferson Ave., 804-818-6889
spottydogicecream.com

Cobra Burger
400 N 27th St., 804-643-8824
cobraburger.com

Sub Rosa Bakery
620 N 25th St., 804-788-7672
subrosabakery.com

GET A TASTE OF RICHMOND'S HISTORY
AT UKROP'S MARKET HALL

No cooking skills required for a nostalgic taste of Richmond's culinary history—simply purchase Ukrop's Homestyle Foods. These family-owned grocery stores served the area from 1937 to 2010, eventually growing to 29 locations in Central Virginia. The stores distinguished themselves with freshly made prepared foods, legendary service (the baggers actually took your groceries to your car, no tipping allowed!), and community involvement. In 1976, the business purchased Dot's Pastry Shop, adding signature bakery products to store shelves, and then added classic Southern recipes from Mrs. Marshall's, another long-time Richmond institution. Over the years, the business's attention to quality and focus on service kept locals loyal. When the Ukrop family sold the grocery stores, they maintained the kitchen. Now, those long-time favorite comfort foods are available from Ukrop's Market Hall and from several regional grocery stores. So for a picnic or other pack-and-go meal, savor the flavor of Richmond nostalgia.

7250 Patterson Ave., 804-340-3040
ukropshomestylefoods.com

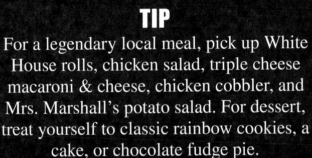

TIP

For a legendary local meal, pick up White House rolls, chicken salad, triple cheese macaroni & cheese, chicken cobbler, and Mrs. Marshall's potato salad. For dessert, treat yourself to classic rainbow cookies, a cake, or chocolate fudge pie.

SPOIL YOUR SWEET TOOTH
AT SHYNDIGZ

Since 2010, Shyndigz has been serving up creative, delicious, generous, and eye-catching desserts. Staples include the cream cheese-frosted Fresh Fruit Cake, Salted Caramel Chocolate Cake, Peanut Butter Pie, Swamp Bar, Lemon Bars, and more—with special cakes, pies, cobblers, and other equally amazing treats sprinkled lavishly into the mix. The business started as a sweet-focused restaurant, and then shifted to a to-go market during the pandemic. Since desserts can be enjoyed anywhere, no table service is needed and business continues to thrive. Conveniently, the owners also operate The Fancy Biscuit nearby, piling Southern-style biscuits with regional staples like country ham and pimento cheese. And if the biscuit spot is closed, look for Fancy Biscuit savory options in Shyndigz's market case. As the business evolves, the attention to scrumptious sweets remains consistent.

1831 W Cary St., 804-938-3449
shyndigz.com

GO WHOLE HOG
AT LA MILPA

The customers and staff at La Milpa restaurant and market attest to its legitimacy. The Spanish language flows as freely as the Mexican food. Plus, it has a heartwarming backstory and an ongoing commitment to culture, tradition, authenticity, and fresh ingredients. Sausages, pork rinds, tortillas, baked goods, and salsas are handcrafted using family recipes. In addition to being a casual counter-service restaurant, La Milpa has a small market of familiar Mexican products. On weekends, it offers a big bonus: a carnitas pop-up, starting with a hog prepared in a massive casserole pot (you might even see the poor porker's head!). The tender, juicy pork is chopped while you wait, served with tacos and house-made toppings, or packaged to go by the pound. Now that's fresh! The Carnitas Tianguis Show pop-up runs Saturdays and Sundays from 9 a.m. to 1 p.m. (get there early—it sells out quickly).

6925 Hull St. Rd., 804-276-3391
lamilparestaurant.com

DINE IN HISTORY
AT THE JEFFERSON

Pair two Richmond favorites—the past and repasts—in restaurants residing in historic buildings. At the most noteworthy of these, Lemaire at the Jefferson Hotel, you can enjoy fine dining and classic regional dishes as artfully plated as they are delicious. The Jefferson also presents Champagne Sunday brunch and afternoon tea for elegant food and experiences. Local tobacco baron Lewis Ginter built the opulent grand hotel in the Spanish Baroque Style and opened it to the public on October 31, 1895. Richmond sculptor Edward V. Valentine created a life-size image of Thomas Jefferson from Carrara marble for the lobby, which also boasts nine original stained-glass Tiffany windows. Contrary to urban legend, the hotel was not used in any *Gone with the Wind* scenes. The lobby pool, however, truly was home to live alligators. Many other restaurants capitalize on the past by inhabiting storied venues, including historic tobacco warehouses, bygone businesses, and heritage houses.

Lemaire at the Jefferson Hotel
101 W Franklin St., 804-649-4629
lemairerestaurant.com

OTHER RESTAURANTS IN HISTORIC BUILDINGS

Old Original Bookbinder's Seafood & Steakhouse
The restaurant traces its history to post–Civil War Philadelphia,
but it's now housed in Richmond's Shockoe Bottom, in the
1901 American Cigar Building in Tobacco Row.
2306 E Cary St., 804-643-6900
bookbindersrichmond.com

The Tobacco Company Restaurant
Elegance and antiques transform the exposed brick, beams,
and columns of an 1866 tobacco warehouse. A three-story
atrium creates a spacious feel. Offering fine dining, a bar,
and live music.
1201 E Cary St., 804-782-9555
thetobaccocompany.com

TAKE YOUR TASTE BUDS TO THE TROPICS
AT CARENA'S

Besides bringing the islands to Richmond, Carena Ives, owner of Carena's Jamaican Grill and Jamaica House, has taken Richmond to the national airwaves. Guy Fieri featured the restaurant on *Diners, Drive-Ins and Dives*, highlighting the Jamaican fried chicken and oxtail stew. Then he invited Ives to compete on *Guy's Grocery Games*, which she won. Employees shared her winnings, but customers triumph each time they eat at her restaurants. Ives learned her craft growing up in Jamaica and brings the island's style and ingredients to her menus: conch fritters, jerk wings, rum-glazed baby back ribs, salmon in creamy coconut sauce, curry goat, whole snapper, and more. Carena's Jamaican Grille provides a sit-down experience and full bar. Jamaica House offers a more casual experience of counter ordering with seating. "Eat well, have a drink, and relax," suggests Carena's menu. "In Jamaica, it's the law!"

Carena's Jamaican Grille
7102 Midlothian Tpk., 804-422-5375
carenasrva.com

Jamaica House
416 W Broad St., 804-358-5793
jamaicahouserva.com

GET A TASTE OF CUBAN CUISINE
AT KUBA KUBA

If traveling to Cuba isn't on your itinerary, Cuban-born Manny Mendez will bring its flavors to you. From appetizers to desserts, Kuba Kuba has been dishing out generous portions of authentic, Cuban-inspired dishes since 1998. The small, friendly, casual atmosphere has a neighborly feel. Hearty, ever-popular paella, with seafood, chorizo, vegetables, and pasta options, demonstrates Cuba's Spanish heritage. Look for eggs all day, roast pork, empanadillas, deep-fried plantains, grilled fish, Cuban coffee and sodas, and, yes, a Cuban sandwich. Oh, and for dessert, the meringue topping on the tres leches cake can't be beat! Mendez opened a West End location in 2015, making Cuban fare more accessible to even more of Richmond.

Kuba Kuba
1601 Park Ave., 804-355-8817
kubakuba.info

Kuba Kuba Dos
403 N Ridge Rd., 804-288-0681
kubakuba.info/kubakubados

FIND THE ANSWER TO RVA BEER AND VIETNAMESE FARE
AT MEKONG AND THE ANSWER

One man and his restaurants have made an impressive mark on Richmond craft beer and Vietnamese dining. Immigrant An Bui came with his family to the US after fleeing Vietnam in 1986. His family opened Mekong restaurant in 1995, and Bui hit upon a novel idea: pair authentic Vietnamese food with great beer—starting with Belgian beers, ideal for pairing. The concept—along with Bui's welcoming attitude, affable family bartenders, and a masterfully curated beer list—attracted a growing crowd of beer fans, giving Mekong a "Cheers!" from beer lovers. Richmond's beer scene fermented here while customers of all drinking persuasions simply enjoyed authentic Vietnamese cuisine. In 2014, Bui opened The Answer Brewpub next door, specializing in IPAs, stouts, and "Joose" sweet and sour fruited beers. The brewpub serves Vietnamese-American food, and 56 taps pour beers brewed on-site alongside guest beers. Beer IS The Answer!

Mekong Restaurant
6004 W Broad St., 804-288-8929
mekongisforbeerlovers.com

The Answer
6008 W Broad St., 804-282-1248
theanswerbrewpub.com

FOLLOW
THE RICHMOND BEER TRAIL

Libations have historic roots and modern sensibilities in Virginia. Early colonial producers, the cultivator of a New World grape, a 19th-century James River Steam Brewery German lagering caves, and the first canned beer all made their mark in the Old Dominion. Today, you'll discover a diversity of beers, like the long-popular Legend Brown, Hardywood Singel, Ardent Pilsner, Isley Choosy Mother peanut butter porter, and Strangeways sours. The Richmond region hosts approximately 40 craft breweries, plus meaderies, distilleries, cideries, wineries, and a seltzer maker. When you want to try various styles from local breweries, start in Scott's Addition, which boasts multiple breweries as well as other craft beverage producers. Then, let the Richmond Beer Trail be your guide. Covering the city and several nearby localities, the trail offers an online listing and map as well as a print map. The guide also indicates which breweries are dog friendly inside and out, which offer food on-site, and which offer other libations. Get your printed trail map stamped at five participating breweries for branded swag. Cheers, Richmond!

The Richmond Beer Trail
visitrichmondva.com/things-to-do/trails/richmond-beer-trail

Richmond West Trail
Breweries, wineries, and distilleries in Goochland and Powhatan counties
richmondwesttrail.com

DON'T WORRY, BE HOPPY
WITH HAZY RICHMOND IPAs

Richmond burst onto the national hazy-IPA radar with the opening of The Veil, thanks to brewer Matt Tarpey's background at both The Alchemist (of Heady Topper fame) and Cantillon Brewery in Belgium. Turns out, other local breweries had also perfected New England–style IPAs as part of their diverse line-ups. At Final Gravity Brewing, brewer and homebrew-shop owner Tony Ammendolia demonstrates his craft with a rotating selection of IPAs. A favorite Triple Crossing beer, Falcon Smash, is available year-round, brewed with wheat for that fuller mouthfeel. Try the hazy IPAs from The Answer or from Väsen Brewing, which uses Norwegian Kveik yeast for extra umph. Stone Brewing, which operates its East Coast location in Richmond, is renowned for IPAs. Richmond breweries offer a diversity of other styles, too, including West Coast-style IPAs, to ensure good cheer.

The Veil Brewing
1509 Belleville St.
4910 Forest Hill Ave.
Funkhaüst Café, 2256 Dabney Rd., Suite F
theveilbrewing.com

Final Gravity Brewing
6118 Lakeside Ave., 804-264-4808
finalgravitybrewing.com

Triple Crossing Beer
113 S Foushee St., 804-495-1955
5203 Hatcher St., 804-729-8707
1101 Winterfield Crossing, Midlothian, 804-495-1955
triplecrossing.com

Väsen Brewing
3331 W Moore St., 804-588-5678
vasenbrewing.com

The Answer
6008 W Broad St., 804-282-1248
theanswerbrewpub.com

Stone Brewing Richmond
4300 Williamsburg Ave.
stonebrewing.com/visit/outposts/richmond

SEE WHAT
THE BUZZ IS ABOUT
WITH MEAD AND CIDER

While beer gets most of the craft love, mead and cider add a delicious dimension to local options. Mead, or honeywine, is a honey-based alcoholic beverage first produced in medieval times. Pollen sources and natural add-ins can generate a host of flavors. Black Heath Meadery established craft mead in Richmond, using Virginia honey, modern techniques, and abundant creativity by adding ingredients like berries, peppers, herbs, and spices, with barrel aging for added complexity. Funktastic Meads expanded the experience, with delightfully big flavors, sessionable meads, and rich wines. Craft cider uses an array of apples, including heritage apples, for ciders from sweet to dry, plus tasty added ingredients. Courthouse Creek Cider offers the ultimate pairing: natural ciders, many made with estate-grown apples and adjuncts, plus house-made gourmet snacks and small plates, house-brewed beer, and wine, all in a peaceful, bucolic rural setting. Buskey Cider is the big-city little brother, with a lively neighborhood vibe.

Black Heath Meadery
1313 Altamont Ave., 804-998-7090
blackheathmeadery.com

Courthouse Creek Cider
1581 Maidens Rd., Maidens, 804-543-3157
courthousecreek.com

Funktastic Meads
1212 Alverser Plz., Midlothian, 804-472-6920
funktasticmeads.com

Buskey Cider
2910 W Leigh St., 804-355-0100
buskeycider.com

Bryant's Cidery & Brewery
2114 E Main St., 804-799-0401
bryantscider.com

GET IN THE SPIRIT
WITH CRAFT DISTILLERIES

The quality of spirits from Richmond distilleries makes it easy to support local. Plus, each one creates different spirits from the others, making it easy to support them all! Many Virginia distilleries operate tasting rooms, too, selling samples, mixed drinks, merchandise, cocktail kits, and their own spirits. Virago Spirits makes a great starting point for exploring distillery tasting rooms, with several liquors appealing to a variety of customers. The comfortable, attractive space features mural-splashed walls, one portraying the business's namesake, Virago, a strong, courageous woman. Bookshelves and armchairs give the room a classic feel. Bartenders mix up creative craft cocktails as well as favorites. Reservoir Distillery specializes in whiskies, from easy-drinking wheat to spicy rye and some aged in a diversity of barrels. The tasting room also emphasizes whiskey education, training staff and providing consumers with nosing and tasting wheels along with ready answers to their questions.

TIP
Distillery tasting rooms are limited in the amount of liquor that they can serve to each customer. Limits are set by Virginia law, not by the distilleries.

Virago Spirits
Flagship Four-Port Rum to high-proof Rum 151, cask-finished rums, gins, and liqueurs
1727 Rhoadmiller St., 804-355-8746
viragospirits.com

Reservoir Distillery
Aged whiskies, including the flagship bourbon, rye, and wheat, each 100 proof and made of 100% corn, rye, and wheat
1800 A Summit Ave., 804-912-2621
reservoirdistillery.com

Cirrus Vodka
Vodka made from 100% potato
1603 Ownby Ln., 804-495-1148
cirrusvodka.com

Belle Isle Craft Spirits
Premium moonshine, including unique flavors like Honey Habanero and Ruby Red Grapefruit
615 Maury St., 804-723-1030
belleislecraftspirits.com

ROLL UP YOUR SLEEVES
AT A COOKING CLASS

Time fries when you're having flan—or some bad dad joke to that effect. Time really will fly when you're learning how to make that delicate dessert, create pasta from scratch, butcher a whole chicken, use a knife correctly, or make the consummate romantic dinner. Richmond's cooking classrooms have the expertise and equipment to lead learners in a variety of kitchen endeavors. Richmond's locally based learning labs are owned and managed by experienced chefs who not only teach their own classes, but bring in other talented professionals to expand the menu. Think cocktail creations, wine pairings, healthy cooking, and a wide diversity of regional and global specialties. While learning to make delightful dishes, students also glean useful take-home cooking tips. Plus, they eat and drink as they learn. Thyme flies, and you will be having fun!

Kitchen Classroom
9018 W Broad St., Henrico, 804-308-3987
thekitchenclassroom.com

Mise En Place
104 Shockoe Slip, 804-404-5328
miseenplacerva.com

WINE DOWN ON THE BANKS OF THE JAMES
AT UPPER SHIRLEY VINEYARDS

Virginia has gained a deserved reputation as a wine destination, from the mountains to the coast. About a half-hour drive from downtown Richmond along scenic Route 5, Upper Shirley Vineyards shows off some of the best wines of the Hampton Roads AVA (American Viticultural Area) using estate-grown grapes, including Petit Verdot, Viognier, Merlot, and Tannat. The tasting room offers a casual but elevated dining menu as well as cocktails and local craft beer. Besides indoor seating, the tasting room has covered porch seating, patios, and a spacious lawn—all with views of the James River and the lush, pristine Presquile National Wildlife Refuge across the wide waterway. The winery also presents live music on weekends. The tasting room is one mile off the Virginia Capital Trail, so you can bike to the winery, on your own bicycle or from a local bike rental company.

Upper Shirley Vineyards
600 Shirley Plantation Rd., Charles City, 804-829-9463
uppershirley.com

James River Cellars Winery
11008 Washington Hwy., Glen Allen, 804-550-7516
jamesrivercellars.com

SAVOR
A PERFECT PAIRING

Much has been made of the art of pairing wine and food—pinky extended, of course. Fortunately, the concept has expanded beyond the carafe. The flavors in craft beers from various malts, hops, and other ingredients complement food, too. And if pairing works with wine and beer, why not cocktails? The bottom line is this: Drink what you want, and eat what you want, at a restaurant that offers the best of both! Two restaurants provide quality food plus well-curated beers, cocktails, and wines. Crafted has 32 draft beers and other drinks to pair with its Southern-inspired menu. Just as a sample: with The Lady Bird chicken sandwich, pair a Pilsner or Riesling; with the Southern Gentleman burger, an IPA or Cabernet; with the Bison Chipotle Meatloaf, a robust porter or Manhattan. Or heck, just order what pairs with your taste buds. It's all there!

Crafted
4900 Libbie Mill East Blvd., 804-554-2738
craftedrva.com

Sedona Tap House
15732 WC Main St., Midlothian, 804-379-0037
5312 Wyndham Forest Dr., Glen Allen, 804-967-3500
sedonataphouse.com

APPRECIATE THE EVOLUTION OF BBQ
AT ZZQ

Many regions stake their claim on barbecue, but Virginia has reason to boast of being the birthplace of the pit-cooked meat—a slow-roasted fusion of indigenous and African American cooking methods with European sauces. Since those early days, Virginia barbecue has embraced influences from elsewhere, too. In fact, one of Richmond's best-loved 'cues comes straight from the heart of Texas. ZZQ pitmaster Chris Fultz was raised in Central Texas. The stacks of lumber and line of commercial cookers beside the restaurant hint at the mouth-watering smoky goodness inside. Treat yourself to ribs, brisket, pulled pork, sausage, or smoked seitan, with stick-to-your-ribs sides like jalapeño mac and cheese, blackstrap collards, terlingua coleslaw, and much more. The always-popular, freshly prepared foods often sell out, and hours are limited, so go early.

3201 W Moore St., 804-528-5648
zzqrva.com

FIND YOUR CHEERS
AT THE JASPER

What do you get when two talented mixologists team up with an experienced restaurateur, all with an appreciation for heritage? You get The Jasper, a bar both sophisticated and approachable. The name pays homage to Jasper Crouch, a Black freedman who was cook and bartender for Chief Justice John Marshall in Richmond in the early 19th century. (Crouch's legendary drink, Quoit Club Punch, is always on the menu.) Creative, modern cocktails mix ingredients in unexpected but brilliant blends, from booziest to refreshing. Liquor lovers can partake of Penicillin Shots, Nitro Bourbon & Ginger, and classic cocktails, too. Or customers can order up a beer—domestic or craft—wine, or a non-alcoholic "tipple" (like the NA-groni!). Food is minimal but satisfying, made to accompany the drinks—not vice versa. In December, stop by for Miracle on Cary. The bar sports its best Christmas décor, music, and themed cocktails. Get there early!

3113 W Cary St.
jasperbarrva.com

TRY THE THREESOME OF BEER, BURGERS, AND ADULT SHAKES
AT STATION 2

A beer, a loaded burger, and a liquor-laden milkshake: the decadent trio satisfies palate, belly, and soul! In Richmond, the OG of the combo is Station 2. Housed in Richmond's old Engine Company 2, built in 1899, Station 2 uses local products, from beef to greens to ice cream. Station 2's trio starts with a carefully curated beer list and presents more than a dozen loaded burgers with options for patty (beef, chicken, turkey, black bean, and Beyond Burger), bread, and side, along with apps and salads. It finishes with decadent adult milkshakes, marrying top-notch Virginia Homestead Creamery ice cream with liquors and other complementary flavors, like orange juice, banana, peanut butter, and chocolate chip. Two other restaurants have their take on the trio, too, for a trio of options.

Beauvine
1501 W Main St.
804-592-5592
beauvineburger.com

Boulevard Burger & Brews
1300 N Arthur Ashe Blvd.
804-367-3838
boulevardburgerandbrew.com

Station 2
2016 E Main St.
804-249-4702
station2richmond.com

GET TWISTED
AT GWARBAR

You could go to GWARbar for the gimmicky décor, a tribute to the Richmond-based heavy metal/hardcore punk band, known for its gory stage show and irreverent humor. You could go for the gruesome heads suspended throughout the restaurant, splashes of faux blood, GWAR memorabilia, and metal music. You could go to pay homage to the band, founded in Richmond in 1985. Or you could go simply for the food. The "intergalactic junk food" presents dive bar meets gourmet: McDuckets made with chicken and duck; freshly ground brisket burgers; vegan Gwartichoke patties; build-your-own mac with an abundance of toppings. While some food names reflect a unseemly spirit—Nachos Destructo, Baconecutioner burger, and Hail Seitan—the kitchen is led by experienced restaurateurs, not by dark copy writers. It's all f'ing good, as Oderus Urungus might sort of say.

217 W Clay St., 804-918-9352
gwarbar.com

CONJURE A BELOVED ITALIAN GRANDMOTHER
AT EDO'S SQUID

The dimly lit stairwell leading up to Edo's Squid is quaint and quiet—it makes you feel as if you're visiting your Nonna's apartment. When you pass through the door at the top of the stairs, though, you step into a lively dining room and are greeted by the scent of fresh garlic. If you get there early, you might even see garlic cloves spread across a table as the staff prepares for another busy night. That's the first sign of the kitchen's use of fresh ingredients. The next sign comes with your first bite of the authentic Italian cuisine. You'll have plenty of choices and hearty portions, in an everyday atmosphere. In addition to nightly specials and lots of seafood, look for ongoing selections, from appetizers, like braised fennel and fried squid, to pasta dishes with marinara and other sauces, with mixed seafood and broccoli rabe and sausage. *Cin! Cin!*

411 N Harrison St., 804-864-5488
edossquidrva.com

CATCH THE SOUL
OF THE CITY

With close to 70 Black-owned restaurants and the annual Richmond Black Restaurant Experience in March, there's plenty of flavor for every palate, especially those that favor soul food. This culinary treasure arose in the South. Enslaved African Americans used ingredients that were easy to forage, grow, or raise. Some cooking methods and ingredients had ties to Africa or were ignored by people with greater resources—like pigs' feet and ears, hog jowl, pork fat, chitlins, and greens. But resourceful cooks knew how to use all available ingredients to make dishes that were tasty and satisfying—so satisfying that they're still popular today. Think fried chicken, fried fish, okra, yams, black-eyed peas, collard greens, and cornbread. Soul food chefs often began learning the craft in their mothers' kitchens, learning family secrets that make the dishes hard to duplicate. But no worries—Richmond's soul food restaurants do the duplicating, so you don't have to.

Southern Kitchen
Traditional soul food staples, including fried chicken and country-fried chicken, meatloaf, pork chops, shrimp 'n' grits, po' boys, and chicken liver
541 N 2nd St., 804-729-4141
southernkitchenrva.net

Mama J's
The matriarch of Richmond's current crop of soul food restaurants, Velma Johnson, serves her comfort soul food
415 N 1st St., 804-225-7449
mamajskitchen.com

Croaker's Spot
Specializing in the seafood, paired with the sweet Croaker's Spot cornbread
1020 Hull St., 804-269-0464
croakersspot.com

Carpenter Theatre at Dominion Energy Center
Credit: Virginia Tourism Corporation

MUSIC
AND ENTERTAINMENT

CATCH A CLASSIC
AT THE CLASSIC BYRD THEATRE

When the 1,200-seat Byrd Theatre opened in 1928, moviegoing was about the experience as well as the film. One of the era's ornate "movie palaces," the Byrd was an American Versailles. The interior featured a royal color scheme, ornate molded plaster, classical murals, and a 2½-ton chandelier with hundreds of concealed lightbulbs with changing colors. It also boasted a Mighty Wurlitzer organ, ascending from the orchestra pit for performances. Now a state and national historic landmark, the theater retains its original glory, while restored and enhanced. It shows second-run films and timeless classics, and it hosts special programs: the *Big Lebowski*-inspired Big LeBYRDski Fest; showings of the French, International, and Environmental film festivals; and more. The theater also offers occasional sensory-friendly movie nights with lights up and volume low. When choosing a movie, look for special announcements noting the Mighty Wurlitzer preshow performance.

2908 W Cary St., 804-358-3056
byrdtheatre.org

SEE WHY RICHMOND IS A HAPPENING PLACE FOR MUSIC
AT THE NATIONAL

Creativity has long wafted in the Richmond air, breeding nationally known entertainment acts, from Bill "Bojangles" Robinson to GWAR, Lamb of God, Jason Mraz, D'Angelo, and Aimee Mann. Local favorites still draw longtime fans: No BS! Brass Band, Lucy Dacus, Bio Ritmo, The Taters, Plunky & Oneness, MoDebree, and more. Eager fans lure in touring musicians, too. While music lovers can find their beat at many venues around the area, The National arguably provides the best package. The venue showcases its elegant 1923 theater décor, a large stage, and state-of-the-art sound system, and it welcomes a diversity of performers. Sightlines are clean, with video screens to supplement the experience. Head to the balcony for seats or to the first floor to stand, and grab drinks and pizza at one of The National's bars.

708 E Broad St., 804-612-1900
thenationalva.com

LAUGH UNTIL YOU CRY
AT LOCAL COMEDY VENUES

Who needs Drew Carey, anyway? Richmond has its own improvisational comedy troupes! Richmond's unofficial "Second City," Coalition Theater, offers classes in stand-up, sketch, and improv as well as opportunities to watch student "recitals" and shows by the pros. Another local franchise, ComedySportz, also offers classes and performances, including family-focused shows. For improv students, improvisational skills contribute to public speaking prowess, team building, communicating with people experiencing dementia, and just plain fun. For audiences, shows are a chance to offer suggestions to the troupes and partake of laughter, that best of medicines. Stand-up performances and open mics around town, often at breweries, add to Richmond's comedy scene. Professional stand-up acts come to Richmond as well, to Funny Bone as well as larger performing arts venues. Whose line is it? Yes, and . . . it's yours!

Coalition Theater
8 W Broad St., 804-420-2271
rvacomedy.com

ComedySportz, Richmond
8906-H W Broad St., 804-266-9377
cszrichmond.com

Richmond Funny Bone
11800 W Broad St., Ste. 1090, 804-521-8900
richmond.funnybone.com

HAVE A
ONE-STOP NIGHT OUT
AT THE TIN PAN

Do you like pairing dinner and a concert for a complete evening out? Keep it simple at The Tin Pan, which presents a complete food menu and a full bar, served at the same table where you'll soak in the music. Waitstaff continue to service you during the show (while respecting the musicians!). Now for the main entrée: the concert. The Tin Pan offers a lineup as diverse as its Tin Pan Alley namesake: folk and Irish folk, bluegrass and blues, funk and soul, jazz and country, world music, and classical. Local acts and touring stars hit the stage to spotlight covers and original music. The venue hosts artists most nights of the week, giving plenty of opportunity to catch a complete night of food and music, all under one welcoming roof.

8982 Quioccasin Rd., 804-447-8189
tinpanrva.com

GET CREATIVE
AT THE VISUAL ARTS CENTER OF RICHMOND

Using creativity can improve mood, boost self-esteem, and relieve stress—even for logical, left-brain thinkers. The Visual Arts Center of Richmond has been helping adults and kids nurture right-brain benefits since 1963. VisArts offers more than 1,000 arts classes each year, from single sessions to multi-week classes, as well as affordable studio access. Participants learn from 200 skilled instructors to work in clay, wood, fiber, painting, photography, printmaking, glass, metal, drawing, creative writing, decorative arts, and other visual media. Special programs include Family Studio for parents and kids and Second Fridays one-night learning sessions. Whether you want to reap right-brain benefits, find a hobby, or explore a new career, VisArts can help you achieve your goals. The center also hosts special exhibitions, so you can appreciate the creativity of other artists, too.

1812 W Main St., 804-353-0094
visarts.org

SURROUND YOURSELF WITH WORLD CULTURE
AT THE RICHMOND FOLK FESTIVAL

You're probably familiar with blues, bluegrass, honky-tonk, zydeco, and gospel music. But how about African *imbube* singing or Puerto Rican *bomba* dancing? Korean *pungmul* and *samulnori* or Indian *Carnatic* classical music? The annual Richmond Folk Festival brings in a diversity of performers from around Virginia, the US, and the world for a three-day celebration of roots music every October. Imagine yourself waltzing along Richmond's historic riverside on a mild autumn day. You settle in to enjoy one group of inspiring performers, and then amble on to another of the six stages. You stop along the way for storytellers, a creative marketplace, demonstrations, kids' activities, adult beverages, and mind-blowing food. Richmond hosted the National Folk Festival from 2005 to 2007. It was such a hit that the city carried it on, and now you can carry it on, too!

Held at Brown's Island and along
the historic riverfront, from 2nd to 7th Streets
richmondfolkfestival.org

TIP

Check the schedule before going to catch the performers that rock your world or for the pre-festival Folk Feast fundraiser. Some stages provide seating, others are bring-your-own chair; some are covered, others are open air. Free, but donations welcome.

GET SWEPT UP IN THE DRAMA
AT A LOCAL THEATER

To laugh, to cry, to think, to dream—local performing arts theaters surround audiences with comedy, drama, and thought-provoking plays and musicals. Performances include world premieres and long-loved classics, featuring professional dues–paying actors, seasoned veterans, and promising new thespians. The region's largest company, Virginia Repertory Theatre, presents locally at three distinctive venues. The Sara Belle and Neil November Theatre operates in the historic Empire Theatre building, erected in 1911 to stage live plays. It became Richmond's first integrated theater after Reconstruction. Barksdale at Hanover Tavern offers an intimate stage at one of the oldest taverns in the US. Licensed in 1733, the tavern served guests such as George Washington and Edgar Allan Poe. The property hosts a restaurant and a pub, for optional preshow sustenance, or simply for dinner. Virginia Rep Center for Arts and Education presents in an old Scottish Rite Masonic Temple on a 650-seat auditorium and two smaller stages.

Virginia Repertory Theatre
804-282-2620
va-rep.org
Virginia Repertory Theatre performs at three distinct venues:

Sara Belle and Neil November Theatre
114 W Broad St.

Barksdale at Hanover Tavern
13181 Hanover Courthouse Rd., Hanover

Virginia Rep Center for Arts and Education
4204 Hermitage Rd.

Swift Creek Mill Theatre
The theatre opened in 1965 inside a charming 300-year-old grist mill. The Mill offers pre-show dinner, too, with menus inspired by the performances, for an easy pleasing evening of dinner and a show. Or just a show or just dinner.
17401 Rte. 1, South Chesterfield, 804-748-5203
swiftcreekmill.com

Richmond Triangle Players
The small but welcoming performance venue celebrates and supports the LGBTQ+ community through programming and encouragement of queer artists. In addition to multi-night runs, the theater hosts cabaret, drag, and other entertaining performances.
Robert B. Moss Theatre, 1300 Altamont Ave., 804-346-8113
rtriangle.org

BE ENTERTAINED
AT ORNATE HISTORIC VENUES

Two Richmond venues entice trendy national acts and stellar local arts groups to their classic, historic theaters. Dominion Energy Center hosts traveling performers and local favorites such as the Richmond Symphony Orchestra, Virginia Opera, and Richmond Ballet. Carpenter Theatre at Dominion opened in 1928 as one of several opulent Loew's Theatres. Look up in this Spanish-inspired atmospheric theater to see floating clouds and a blanket of stars twinkling overhead in a midnight-blue ceiling. Look all around, at the elegant walls and rich golden trim, like a lavish Mediterranean courtyard. Altria Theater attracts spectacular traveling Broadway shows and a diversity of national touring acts. Altria Theater opened in 1927, built by the Shriners in a Moorish Revival style. Décor features an abundance of ornamental tile, towering minarets, and desert murals. At Dominion or Altria, go early so you can enjoy the venue before the main event.

Altria Theater
6 N Laurel St., 804-592-3384
altriatheater.com

Dominion Energy Center
600 E Grace St., 804-592-3330
dominionenergycenter.com

LEARN THROUGH FUN
AT THE CHILDREN'S MUSEUM
OF RICHMOND

Dishing out a heaping helping of play alongside generous servings of learning, the Children's Museum of Richmond offers hours of fun for kids and their adults. Multisensory experiences engage all the senses in purposeful play and creative art projects. Interactive exhibits highlight age-appropiate lessons in familiar, kid-sized settings: mini restaurants and grocery stores, farm animals, banking, TV broadcasting, trains, trees, caverns, and more! The inside is bright and airy, and the outside features active play areas. CMoR offers special programs, including monthly sessions for children with disabilities, bilingual signage and story times, and sensory backpacks. Oh, and there are lots of tips for adults on engaging with kids, too, as well as chances to play along. The museum celebrates the diversity of children and their cultural traditions, so kids can, too. The museum is tailored for children through the age of 8 years old. Check the calendar for even more fun times.

Children's Museum of Richmond
2626 W Broad St., 804-474-7000

CMoR Chesterfield
6629 Lake Harbour Dr., Midlothian, 804-474-7000

childrensmuseumofrichmond.org

HAVE A WILD, AWW-MAZING TIME
AT THE METRO RICHMOND ZOO

There's nothing like an adorable animal to elicit smiles and to open hearts and minds. At the 150-acre Metro Richmond Zoo, the "oohs," "ahhs," and "awws" serve a greater purpose: to educate and inspire visitors toward the long-term mission of protecting animals around the world. The privately owned zoo is accredited by the Zoological Association of America and supports conservation efforts through financial contributions and award-winning breeding programs. Guests can get a gander of animals large and small, representing 190 species: tigers, bears, birds, reptiles, bats, monkeys, and more. Catch a glimpse of zoo babies, including young pygmy hippos, cheetahs, snow leopards, orangutans, and penguins. As one young guest said of the meerkats, "They're so frickin' cute!" For a different perspective, guests can hop on the zoo train, the aerial chairlift, or the Adventure Park zipline, including zips over animal enclosures. Gaze, engage, and learn!

8300 Beaver Bridge Rd., Moseley, 804-739-5666
metrorichmondzoo.com

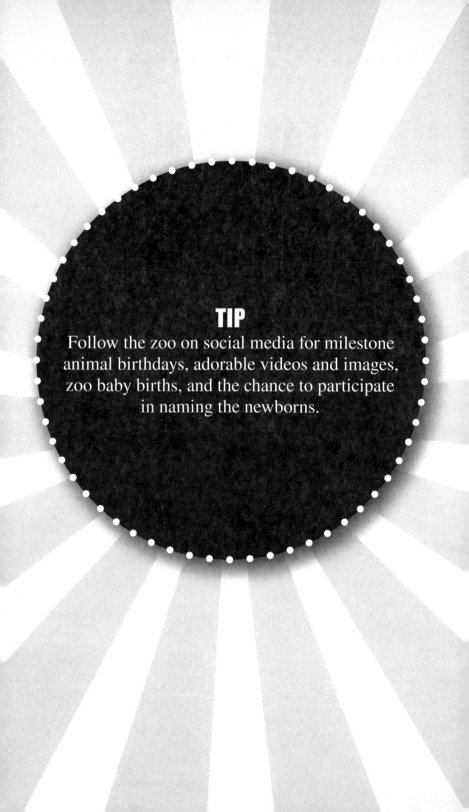

TIP

Follow the zoo on social media for milestone animal birthdays, adorable videos and images, zoo baby births, and the chance to participate in naming the newborns.

EAT, DRINK, AND BE MERRY
ALL UNDER ONE ROOF

Adult-focused game venues have been dropping into Richmond like tiles in Tetris. Arcade games, shuffleboard, bowling, bocce, mini golf—play these games inside, year-round, while eating, drinking, and hanging out. Most allow kids but also enforce adults-only hours. If you and your fun-loving companions value food, drink, and amusement, all three, aim for Bingo Beer Co. The beer is brewed onsite by an experienced brewer who cranks out everything from a clean, crushable lager to a hazy IPA, a fruity sour to a complex Brett beer, a rich stout to a smoked bock. The food menu was crafted by experienced restaurateurs and presents pub food with pizzazz. Plus the full bar serves creative and classic cocktails as well as wine. Entertainment goes far beyond the venue's previous life as a bingo hall—classic arcade games offer a winning formula, sure to amp up your fun quotient.

Bingo Beer Co.
2900 W Broad St., 804-386-0290
bingorva.com

The Circuit Arcade Bar
More than 80 games, snacks, and a self-serve tap wall
3121 W Leigh St.
thecircuitarcadebar.com

Slingshot Social Game Club
Bocce, superskee ball, and extreme duckpin, with finger foods
and bar food, full bar, and a self-serve tap wall
3301 W Clay St.
slingshotgameclub.com/location/richmond-va

DraftCade
More than 75 classic arcade games with unlimited game play
for one low price, plus 60 drafts and bar food
11800 W Broad St., #1090, 804-476-2800
draftcade.com/richmond

The Park
Duckpin bowling, miniature golf, virtual golf, a comedy club,
and music, plus food vendors, full bar service, and
a self-serve tap wall
1407 Cummings Dr., 804-533-2966
thepark.com

CATCH A PERFORMANCE
AT FIREHOUSE THEATRE

Creativity is sparked for audiences and participants alike at Firehouse Theatre. The performing arts venue sprang from the ashes when Richmond Fire Department's Station House #10 was decommissioned. Five local theater artists transformed the building into a performance space, supported by a nonprofit. Rather than simply putting on its own shows, the nonprofit decided to provide a home for creativity to thrive. The firehouse-turned-stage hosts new and established plays, poetry, comedy, magic, dance, music, creative work sessions, and more. Productions may be wholesome, like Firehouse Radio Players' stage re-creations of old radio shows. They may be edgy, as in Firehouse Fringe—unconventional, unorthodox, avant-garde. Performers may be local or from afar. Given the bountiful, diverse calendar of events, you're sure to find something to set your spirit on fire.

1609 W Broad St., 804-355-2001
firehousetheatre.org

DANCE LIKE YOU'RE IN THE TROPICS
AT HAVANA '59

It's easy to envision yourself in Cuba at Havana '59. Inside and out, the restaurant and bar has been decked out in the style of an old Cuban building, including crumbling plaster, palm trees, string lights, and a neon marquee to punctuate the ambience of the West Indies. The Cuban cuisine, fresh tropical cocktails, and cigar bar enhance the aura. But on Thursdays, the atmosphere rocks with a rhythmic tropical feel. Salsa music and a generous dance floor invite all comers to spin, shimmy, and step along. Don't know how to dance salsa? No problem! The restaurant offers one-hour dance lessons, presenting both salsa and bachata. Transport yourself, body and soul, to 1950s Havana, when the city was known as Paris of the Caribbean. "Bailar con Nosotros"—"Dance with Us"—Havana '59 proclaims!

16 N 17th St., 804-780-2822
havana59.com

GET IN THE CHRISTMAS SPIRIT
WITH RICHMOND'S HOLIDAY LIGHTS

Colonial Williamsburg, an hour east of Richmond, claims to have popularized the holiday tradition of white lights in windows. The practice spread to Richmond, which also celebrated colonial architecture, colors, and customs. White lights still grace many local houses, presenting a gentle glow of hospitality. But other traditions light up the city, too, including houses festooned with colored bulbs and seasonal displays. To make the most of these traditions, take a tacky light tour—drive it yourself or with a local tour company. Wander through two historic Richmond neighborhoods, Church Hill and the Fan, both decked out for the occasion. Official walking tours are offered as well as DIY holiday strolls. Several restaurants and bars throw a month-long party, with holiday-themed drinks and food and high-proof décor, including Miracle on Cary at The Jasper and The Jefferson's Lemaire restaurant. In the darkest weeks of the year, Richmond lights up the town.

Discover Richmond Tours
discoverrichmondtours.com

CELEBRATE FABULOUS DIVERSITY
AT GODFREY'S DRAG BRUNCH

Brunch never felt so fabulous! Every weekend, Godfrey's opens its doors to spirited crowds who dine on delicious brunch foods and drinks while cheering on some of the best drag queens from Richmond and beyond. Godfrey's was showcasing female illusionists even before RuPaul popularized the art form. The performers' energy and joy attract a diverse audience—the talented, dressed-to-the-nines queens work the crowd, making everyone a welcome part of the show. The rest of the week, Godfrey's nightclub space opens its arms to LGBTQ+ revelers and allies, dishing out DJs, dancing, music, and more drag shows. One weeknight focuses on young adult visitors, 18 and up, giving youth a place to feel safe and included.

308 E Grace St., 804-549-9512
godfreysva.com

TIP

Reservations are required and fill fast. Brunch performances are for all ages but recommended as PG-13. Be sure to have dollar bills on hand to tip the performers as they dance.

PUTTER AWAY YOUR TIME
AT HOTEL GREENE

Discard that image of miniature golf as a kids' game. Instead of windmills and loop-de-loops, picture yourself tapping a ball through an early 20th-century hotel, posh but with ominous signs of decay. Bump your golf ball around the tiled columns of a public bathhouse, past peepholes into a long-gone world, and down a hallway lined with closed doors. Bounce it off bumpers in a stylized guest room with a brass bed and portmanteau, and through a library of leatherbound books. Imagine, too, the drink you're toting along: a craft cocktail, beer, or wine. Perhaps your 13 rounds of golf come after—or before—dining in the Hotel Greene's lobby. You won't be staying the night at this "fauxtel," but given its haunting tales, you probably wouldn't want to.

508 E Franklin St.
hotelgreene.com

PARTY
AT RICHMOND'S LONGEST-RUNNING CONCERT SERIES, FRIDAY CHEERS

For two months each year, Richmond counts on a big party every Friday. The party fills Brown's Island, downtown's premier, open-air event space. Bands perform on one end of the island, and spectators spread out along the grassy lawn—dancing, standing, or reclining on blankets and portable chairs. A train may rumble along the tracks above the island, offering sound effects appropriate to the lyrics. Local food and beverage vendors keep partygoers satiated. The diversity of musicians, including some locals, reflects Richmond's diverse population. Bands range from alt-country and indie to jazz and funk, like Zac Brown Band, Tyler Childers, and The Head and the Heart to Lucy Dacus and Tank and the Bangas. Early summer dates, spanning May and June, make for beautiful weather, often moderate temperatures under a big, blue-sky canopy. Since the 1980s, the annual concert series has been entertaining people of all ages—including yours.

Hosted by Venture Richmond on Brown's Island
venturerichmond.com/our-events/friday-cheers

FILL YOUR MIND WITH ARTS
AT UR AND VCU

At a university, youthful exuberance meets blooming creativity and exploding intellectual growth. So what better place to catch an abundance of arts? From student shows and recitals to special guest appearances, Richmond's two largest universities showcase diverse works that will make you smile, appreciate, and think. Feed your curiosity with music, dance, visual arts, theater, and lectures. The Modlin Center for the Arts at the University of Richmond is the one-stop shop for arts at UR. The university is its own showcase of collegiate Gothic architecture on a rolling landscape, so allow extra time to stroll the idyllic campus. Several venues host arts at Virginia Commonwealth University. Its urban location means easy access to dinner or drinks before or after the show.

Modlin Center for the Arts at University of Richmond
435 Westhampton Way, University of Richmond, 804-289 8980
modlin.richmond.edu

VCUarts
804-VCU-ARTS
The Anderson, 907½ W Franklin St.
Institute for Contemporary Art, 601 W Broad St.
W. E. Singleton Center for Performing Arts, 922 Park Ave.
Dance Center, 10 N Brunswick St.
arts.vcu.edu/events

LET THE MUSIC STRING YOU ALONG
WITH THE RICHMOND SYMPHONY

Don't let the stodgy reputation of symphonic music throw you.
The Richmond Symphony plays outside the lines. Sure, it still
showcases the masters and contemporary composers, especially
with performances by the full orchestra, but the talented
musicians also embrace contemporary pop music, like playing
the tunes of *Star Wars: The Return of the Jedi* in concert with
the film, presenting tango music accompanied by tango dancers,
toting their instruments to a brewery for chamber classics paired
with craft beer and pizza, presenting "Carnival of the Animals"
to elementary school students and serenading visitors to the
Virginia Museum of Fine Arts. If classical music is your jam,
you'll find lots to love. But if not, the Richmond Symphony
might open your mind, and you just might wonder where this
music has been "Haydn" all your life.

Various venues, check website for schedule or call 804-788-1212
richmondsymphony.com

The James River and Belle Isle
Credit: Annie Tobey

SPORTS
AND RECREATION

TRAVERSE THE TRAILS
OF THE JAMES RIVER PARK SYSTEM

Just a few blocks from downtown, the James River Park System greets visitors with greenspaces and old-growth forests, easy footpaths, and technical trails. Sounds of water splashing over rocks and birds chattering, blue heron and osprey sightings, and the calls of insects drown out reminders of nearby city streets. The 600-acre park straddles the river and offers more than 40 miles of diverse trails—amazing for mountain bikers, trail runners, or walkers—plus water access for fishing, boating, swimming, and rock hopping. Sections of the park stretch from Huguenot Flatwater in the west (with an accessible kayak launch) to historic Ancarrow's Landing in the east. Highlights include the old stone Pump House, Pipeline Walkway, Buttermilk and North Bank singletrack trails, a climbing wall, the Flood Wall walkway, the historic Belle Isle, and wild pawpaw fruit in early fall.

jamesriverpark.org

TIP

The park system is free. It offers an abundance of access points and parking, but minimal amenities—scattered porta-potties, trash receptacles (leave no trace!), and a few year-round drinking fountains— so carry hydration and wear appropriate shoes.

45

"HAVE FUNN AND GO NUTS"
WITH THE FLYING SQUIRRELS

The Richmond Flying Squirrels baseball team may not play major league ball, but it has major league fun at minor league prices. Fans catch professional sports alongside hilarious, high-energy entertainment between innings. The "funn" is led by mascot Nutzy and his sidekick, Nutasha, and by the colorful Squirrels' CEO, Todd "Parney" Parnell. Games at The Diamond stadium include theme nights, fireworks, pint-sized fun, and special promotions; special nights highlight kids, Latin American fans, and fans with disabilities; giveaways range from T-shirts to bobbleheads; and vendors hawk food and drinks—including a wide selection of local craft beer in generous servings at easy prices. You don't have to love sports to go nuts over the Double-A Affiliate of the San Francisco Giants. You only have to love having fun.

The Richmond Flying Squirrels at The Diamond
3001 N Arthur Ashe Blvd., 804-359-3866
milb.com/richmond

FIND A PARK LOVER'S PARADISE
AT POCAHONTAS STATE PARK

An easy half-hour drive from downtown Richmond lies Virginia's largest state park, a forested oasis for staying or playing. Go fishing or boating on Swift Creek Lake; swim in the aquatic center pools; have a picnic; get smarter at the Civilian Conservation Corps Museum or nature center; or explore the park's 90 miles of trails, from easy to technical, for hiking, trail running, horseback riding, and mountain biking. Pocahontas has more than 44 miles of dedicated directional mountain bike trails, including single-track and accessible hand-cycle friendly trails. Wildlife appreciate the park, too: songbirds, waterfowl, deer, chipmunks, and frogs provide a chorus of night sounds as you drift off to sleep in your RV, tent, Yurt, or rental cabin. Follow the park's calendar for Pocahontas Premieres concerts, educational programs, and sports competitions. The park's accessibility features make this dose of nature therapy a win for everyone.

10301 State Park Rd., Chesterfield
dcr.virginia.gov/state-parks/pocahontas

TIP
Download a free park trail map on the Avenza Maps app for real-time GPS location.

GET A KICK
OUT OF THE RICHMOND KICKERS

As the longest continuously running professional soccer club in the country (pun intended), the Richmond Kickers have been firing up Richmonders since 1993. The club's games are the best-attended in the USL League One, stoking eager fans with their energy and verve. It helps, too, that City Stadium offers more than just high-octane soccer. It's a great place to hang out with family and friends, to eat, drink, and be spirited. Kickers' fans can choose among multiple concessions, including popular local food trucks and a wide selection of craft beer, wine, and seltzers. A wide terrace behind the stands offers space for vendors and visiting. The games are dog friendly, too! To Ted Lasso's AFC Richmond: Eat your hearts out. Thanks to Kickers' football, we really are Richmond.

Richmond Kickers at City Stadium
3201 Maplewood Ave.
richmondkickers.com

CRUISE
THE VIRGINIA CAPITAL TRAIL

Any given day brings plenty of bikers, walkers, and runners out to the Virginia Capital Trail—especially on the picture-perfect-weather days. With 51.7-miles of dedicated paved pathway, crowds are never an issue. The Virginia Capital Trail reaches from Great Shiplock Park in downtown Richmond to Jamestown Settlement. Users can tackle a few miles or many, buffered safely from the roadway. Travelers pass bucolic scenery, woods, fields, wetlands and waterways, scattered restaurants and stores, a winery, parks, and historical sites, including the entrance to the 19th-century James River Steam Brewery beer caves. The rural route means plenty of bird choruses and occasional critters along the way. No motorized vehicles are allowed, but you can also traverse the trail on skates, handcycles, or electric bikes. Whatever your mode of transport, it's always smart to pack water, phone, sunscreen, snacks, ID, and money or credit card.

Virginia Capital Trail
virginiacapitaltrail.org

Richmond Trailheads
Great Shiplock Park, 2803 Dock St.
Dorey Park, 2999 Darbytown Rd., Henrico
Four Mile Creek Trailhead, 3256 New Market Rd, Henrico

NO BIKE? NO PROBLEM! RENT A BIKE, OR RENT AN ELECTRIC BIKE, FOR ALL THE FUN WITH LESS OF THE WORK.

Adventures in RVA
1912 E Main St., 804-648-2453
rvabikerental.com

Kul Wheels Electric Bikes
1106 New Market Rd., 804-205-3452
kulwheels.com

The Kickstand
3011 Water St.
richmondcyclingcorps.org/kickstand

TRAVERSE FOUR UNIQUE TRAILS
ALONG THE JAMES

Four distinctive routes along the river in downtown Richmond provide opportunities to soak in both nature and history: the Pipeline, Floodwall, Canal Walk, and T. Pott Bridge. The Pipeline is a metal catwalk that runs on top of a storm pipe, below a train trestle, and over the river. The walkway along the Floodwall Park offers elevated views of the city and of wildlife, including great blue herons, osprey, and bald eagles. The Floodwall trail meets with the T. Tyler Potterfield Memorial Bridge, built atop a former hydroelectric dam. The paved Canal Walk shows off historic structures, modern murals, bronze historical marker medallions, a cross marking the 1607 arrival of British explorers, a wall illustrating the city's highest floodwater marks, and a monument to Henry Box Brown, who escaped slavery in a wooden crate. With unique walks like this, you'll meet your step goals without even knowing it.

TIPS

The trails can be combined into one loop route, though planned reconstruction of the 14th Street Bridge will temporarily obstruct the east end of the loop. The Potterfield Bridge and Canal Walk are universally accessible. Some dogs are intimidated by the Potterfield Bridge because of its surface and its closeness to the rapids. The Floodwall is universally accessible from the western end only. The Pipeline, accessed on one end by a metal ladder, is neither handicap accessible nor dog friendly.

Pipeline Walk
End of South 12th St., small parking lot
jamesriverpark.org/explore-the-park-pipeline

Canal Walk
Access points at nearly every block between 5th and 17th Streets, with universally accessible entrances at 5th, 10th, 12th, 14th, and 16th.
venturerichmond.com/explore-downtown/riverfront-canal-walk

T. Tyler Potterfield Memorial Bridge
From Belle Isle parking lot near Brown's Island: Tredegar St.,
jamesriverpark.org/t-tyler-potterfield-memorial-bridge

Floodwall Park
South end of the 14th Street Bridge, small parking lot
jamesriverpark.org/explore-the-park-floodwall-park

CHILL OUT, WORK OUT, OR ROCK OUT
AT DOMINION RIVERROCK

Surrounded by fresh spring air, the rushing river, and plenty of adrenaline, spectators and competitors alike get pumped at Dominion Riverrock. For casual adventurers and hardcore enthusiasts, the family- and dog-friendly event rocks a weekend of fun. Participants can compete in fishing, trail running, and photography, as well as in skilled sports like mountain biking, bouldering, whitewater paddling, and the multi-sport team adventure race. Casual spectators can try an array of experiences—stand-up paddleboarding, bouldering, slackline, kayaking—all for free. Guests can take an outdoor yoga class, watch the "ultimate air dogs" spring from the dock into the pool, grab some food and drink from one of the many vendors, spread a blanket on the ground, and rock to the free live music. Adrenaline junkie or not, anyone can join in the celebration of Richmond's great outdoors in the city.

A Sports Backers event, held at Brown's Island
riverrockrva.com

REV UP YOUR ENGINES
AT RICHMOND RACEWAY

If you're already a fan of auto racing, you'll dig the Richmond Raceway. If you aren't, you just might discover that the roar of the engines and the enthusiasm of the crowds get your adrenaline pumping. The Richmond racetrack is three-quarters of a mile long, dubbed America's Premier Short Track. Its unique "D" shape allows drivers to reach high speeds along the 1,290-foot front stretch. Races include NASCAR appearances two weekends each year, high-energy races like the NASCAR Cup Series, Xfinity Series, the Whelen Modified Touring Series, and the Craftsman Truck Series. Richmond racing couldn't happen without the fans, so Richmond Raceway works to provide first-class amenities and fan experiences: Kids Zone, special FanGrounds, mega Midway action, and driver Q&As. Fans can complete their experience with on-site RV and tent camping.

600 E Laburnum Ave., 866-455-7223
richmondraceway.com

RUN WITH A GANG ...
OF RUNNERS
WITH SPORTS BACKERS AND RRRC

In Richmond, you can lace up your shoes to run on roads and trails. If you enjoy running with other people—for safety, camaraderie, or to learn more about the city and its running routes—RVA has plenty of opportunities. Locals and visitors alike can drop in on informal organized groups targeted for parts of town or other metrics. The Richmond Road Runners Club (RRRC) maintains a list of themed routes and public running groups: road and trail, speedy and casual, plus affinity groups such as RVA Stroller Runners, Black Men Run, brewery running clubs, and more. Looking for a race? Go to the RRRC website's Race Calendar tab for races big and small, short and long, for a cause and just for fun. Or see what Sports Backers has coming up, like the Monument Avenue 10k, Uncorked Half and 5k winery run, or the fall Richmond Marathon, Half, and 8k. In Richmond, you never need to run alone.

Richmond Sports Backers
sportsbackers.org

Richmond Road Runners Club
rrrc.org

GO FISH
ON THE JAMES

The James River ranked #1 in Virginia for citation smallmouth bass catches reported in 2022. Conveniently, most of the James that runs through Richmond is open to public access. "Anglers should target transition areas where deep runs and pools meet shallow rocky riffles," advises the Virginia Department of Wildlife Resources. Late winter and early spring are optimal for smallmouth bass in pre-spawn mode, and floating the James is the best way to cover the waterway. As the weather warms, key in on riffles breaks created by boulders and debris. Richmond-based angler John Bryan recommends fishing for shad in April, beneath the 14th Street Bridge, the terminus of the rapids. To fish with children, hop the dry rocks south of Belle Isle and drop a line in the pools and currents that run between the rocks. For fly fishing, head upriver to Pony Pasture. Know the fishing regulations and license requirements before casting your line.

Virginia Department of Wildlife Resources
dwr.virginia.gov/fishing/regulations

GO MOUNTAIN BIKING ON THE REGION'S TRAILS
WITH RIVERSIDE CYCLING

Imagine yourself biking on wooded trails, accompanied by bird songs and the splash of water over rocks. The region's mountain biking trails offer just such experiences. From technical trails—with rocks, roots, steep inclines, and twisty turns—to flat and easy. Pocahontas State Park has more than 44 miles of dedicated mountain bike trails, some handcycle friendly. The James River Park System boasts nearly 20 miles of shared trails. Smaller parks offer cycling experiences, too, like Leake's Mill Park in Goochland and Poor Farm Park in Ashland. No experience? No bike? No worries! Riverside Cycling offers rentals, sales, and even lessons. Instructors can meet you at your level, from learning to navigate trails to tackling technical features. They can even bring a bike to you. Put your imagination in motion!

3 Manchester Rd., 804-496-0226
riversidecyclingrva.com

TIP
Check RVA Trail Report on Facebook before heading out for updates on conditions and to avoid damaging soggy trails.

GET CARRIED AWAY
ON THE JAMES RIVER
WITH RIVERSIDE OUTFITTERS

The river rapids stretch seven miles along the James, ending at the city of Richmond. The adrenaline rush blends with sights serene and impressive, past miles of woodlands, fields, wildlife, parks, historic structures, and Richmond's skyline. While about six miles of rapids are gentle (class I to II), the last half-mile sees the steepest drop, creating challenging rapids (class II to IV) and thrills for whitewater enthusiasts. Above and below the rapids, the waterway flows unobstructed, making it delightful for tubing and stand-up paddleboarding. The experienced paddlers at Riverside Outfitters can help guests navigate the river whatever their comfort level, offering guidance and lessons, rental crafts, and guided adventures. Best of all, the river's proximity to the city makes for an easy transition from water fun to creature comforts.

Riverside Outfitters
6836 Old Westham Rd., 804-560-0068
riversideoutfitters.com

RVA Paddlesports
1511 Brook Rd., 804-898-0697
rvapaddlesports.com

TIP
The river's hazards include the dangerous Z-Dam, Bosher's Dam, and other challenges. Know the hazards, the river level, and the weather before you get on the water. Check jamesriverpark.org/riversafety for tips, or go with experienced James River paddlers.

CLIMB THE WALL
AT THE OLD MANCHESTER BRIDGE

Richmond may not have mountains, but its rich recreational scene has sparked the creativity of outdoor enthusiasts who have discovered and made a multitude of climbing and bouldering opportunities. At the Manchester Climbing Wall, climbers scale an abandoned granite bridge abutment. Other challenges await an easy hike away: climb the granite walls at the Belle Isle Quarry or the stone wall at Oregon Hill or go bouldering along the Buttermilk Trail, Forest Hill Park, the Cove, and Pony Pasture. If you're new to the sport, you can learn the ropes at Peak Experiences climbing gyms. The facilities' 100+ top rope routes, lead-only areas, auto-belays, and bouldering walls have routes crafted for beginners and advanced climbers. The long-time locals at Peak Experiences can teach novice climbers and help climbers of all levels discover the many opportunities to climb high in RVA.

Peak Experiences
11421 Polo Cir., Midlothian, 804-897-6800
1375 Overbrook Rd., 804-655-2628
peakexperiences.com

TAKE A CHILD TO PLAY AND LEARN TO LOVE
AT PARK365

This free, 2.4-acre playground was designed to accommodate individuals with disabilities while welcoming everyone. PARK365 has three separate playgrounds for toddlers, school-aged kids, and every age after that. Visitors can swing, splash in water troughs, play musical instruments, and more. Extra-special features include a wheelchair-accessible treehouse, a multisensory wall with panels stimulating touch, hearing, and sight; handicap-accessible swings and fitness equipment; and charging stations for electric wheelchairs. The space also provides soft safety surfaces, a shaded pavilion with picnic tables, water fountains and misters, and a family restroom. But what makes PARK365 most special is the people. All are welcome, all are welcoming—that's one of the best lessons any child can learn.

3600 Saunders Ave., 804-358-1874
soar365.org/park365

BE PART OF A 2,000-YEAR-OLD TRADITION
AT THE RICHMOND INTERNATIONAL DRAGON BOAT FESTIVAL

These dragons may not breathe fire, but the experience will spark your adrenaline, whether you're watching from the shoreline or firing up your energy as part of the 22-person crew. Your heart can keep time with the team's drummer marking cadence, the piston-like pumping of 20 oars, the calls of the sweep, and the progress of the 40-foot-long boat as it cuts through the water. The Richmond International Dragon Boat Festival each August welcomes novices as well as international competitors. It provides all the equipment, too. Besides being a blast of fun and teamwork, the festival showcases a 2,000-year-old Chinese tradition: the boats boast a dragon head and tail at the bow and stern, and cultural performances punctuate the day. So grab your friends, create your chants, and get out on the water—or just watch!

A Sports Backers event, held at Rocketts Landing
5000 Old Osborne Tpk., 804-285-9495
sportsbackers.org/events/richmond-international-dragon-boat-festival

TREAT YOUR DOG TO A ROMP
AT RUFF CANINE CLUB

If you have a dog, take him to Ruff Canine Club, Richmond's private dog club. Your furry baby can romp with other canines while you feel virtuous about treating him to a fun, safe outing. Unlike most dog parks, Ruff pups are vetted to ensure they have current vaccinations. Behavior is monitored, and misbehaving dogs and owners are asked to leave. The play yard is maintained for cleanliness and safety, with separate areas for small and large dogs. But best of all, the park caters to the parents, too: numerous picnic tables offer seating, where you can relax or enjoy some of the food and beverages available at Ruff, including delicious flatbreads and a nice selection of beers and wines. Ruff Canine Club offers day passes as well as monthly and annual memberships. Register your dog before you go, providing proof of vaccinations and spaying/neutering, and then go get ruff. If you don't have a dog, you can still eat, drink, and be amused at the canine antics.

1924 Ellen Rd., 804-562-2038
ruffcanineclub.com

HAVE A FUN FLING WITH DISC GOLF
AT GILLIE'S CREEK PARK

No matter your age, fitness, or experience level, if you can toss a flying disc (such as a Frisbee), you can play disc golf. Like standard golf, you start at a "tee" and aim for a target, often an elevated metal basket. You make your way down the fairway, surrounded by nature, getting light exercise along the way. Equipment is minimal—you really only need one decent disc, which costs about $15—and it's often free to play, with no other special equipment or tee times needed. Several public parks in the Richmond area have popular disc golf courses, all free. The Gillie's Creek Park course is especially beginner friendly, with 17 of its 18 holes under 300 feet, on flat terrain. Plus, it offers a view of the city's skyline. The park is located near downtown, near Stone Brewing and Triple Crossing Beer, for a 19th hole.

4425 Williamsburg Ave.
rva.gov/parks-recreation/gillies-creek-park

TIP
Gillie's Creek Park is also home to a BMX racetrack and horseshoe pits.

OTHER PARKS TO ENJOY

Joseph Bryan Park
A more challenging course in a beautiful setting, with a mix of hole lengths, elevation changes, and trees and ponds poised to intercept your disc; the park also has walking trails and stocked ponds
4308 Hermitage Rd.
dwr.virginia.gov/waterbody/bryan-park

Dorey Park
Recreational but challenging, with a mix of hole lengths and open and tight holes; accessible from the Virginia Capital Trail; also has a stocked lake, dog park, horse trails and ring, and other park amenities
2999 Darbytown Rd., Henrico
henrico.us/rec/places/dorey

Truetimber Disc Golf Course
Membership course in a historical wooded setting that offers weekday hours for nonmembers; short holes, but tight and technical
4050 Transport Pl.
facebook.com/truetimberdgc

Emancipation and Freedom monuments on Brown's Island
Credit: Annie Tobey

CULTURE
AND HISTORY

IMMERSE YOURSELF IN RICHMOND'S HISTORY
WITH THE VALENTINE

To understand Richmond's big picture, start at the Valentine Museum. Visitors, newcomers, and long-time locals will find illuminating snapshots of the city's history and culture. Historic artifacts bring life to the story: a carousel horse from an early amusement park, lunch counters that witnessed the city's sit-ins, a Lucky Strike ad, an Eskimo Pie doll, and the paint-splattered statue of Confederate president Jefferson Davis, as he lies after 2020 protests. The museum experience includes the Wickham House next door, offering tours of the early-19th-century home, and the studio of notable sculptor Edward Valentine. The Valentine also operates the First Freedom Center in Shockoe Bottom, which marks Thomas Jefferson's Virginia Statue for Religious Freedom, and offers self-guided tours, seasonal guided walking tours, and special events, all designed to educate and spark positive change.

The Valentine Museum and Wickham House
1015 E Clay St., 804-649-0711
thevalentine.org

The Valentine First Freedom Center
14 S 14th St., 804-649-0711
thevalentine.org/exhibition/first-freedom-center

ENGAGE WITH HISTORY
AT THE VIRGINIA MUSEUM
OF HISTORY & CULTURE

Forget boring history classes and textbooks. The Virginia Museum of History & Culture makes history accessible and relatable. One of the museum's long-term exhibitions, "Our Commonwealth," literally surrounds you with each of Virginia's regions. You'll learn about the landscapes, foodways, industries, culture, and people, from the mountains to the coast. Visually rich and appealing, each sensory-filled room pulls you gently into the region, using moving murals, gentle background sounds, intriguing artifacts, and striking displays. Other museum exhibitions share different aspects of history: "The Story of Virginia," from 16,000 BC to contemporary times; "Taking Aim," highlighting historic firearms; "The Lost Cause," on the years following the American Civil War; and more. The museum also runs short-term exhibitions and special events—lectures, learning, kid stuff, and fun. Pictures, artifacts, and engaging displays add depth to the lessons. History never looked so good!

428 N Arthur Ashe Blvd., 804-340-1800
virginiahistory.org

MARVEL AT WORLDWIDE CREATIVITY, THOUGHTFULNESS, AND BEAUTY
AT THE VMFA

Gaze at the intricacies of a Fabergé egg. Puzzle over a Picasso. Savor the beauty of art by Monet and van Gogh. Salute the inspiration of Kehinde Wiley. Be astonished at the detail in beaded clothing from Native women. Relax beside a cascading fountain and garden sculptures. Learn from an expert. These and other experiences allow art aficionados and casual observers alike to appreciate the priceless collections at the Virginia Museum of Fine Arts—nearly 50,000 works of art from 6,000 years of history. Permanent collections include Chinese, African and African American, French Impressionists, Art Nouveau, Himalayan, and Native American. Special themed exhibitions convey both meaning and artistry in an ever-changing palette. The VMFA is open 365 days a year, with fine dining, a café, a gift shop, and special events. General admission is always free, with cost for some temporary exhibitions. It's all so marvel-ous!

200 N Arthur Ashe Blvd., 804-340-1400
vmfa.museum

EXPLORE A BOUNTY OF FLOWERS AND FUN
AT LEWIS GINTER BOTANICAL GARDEN

A trip to Lewis Ginter Botanical Garden provides a dose of nature's medicine, compounded with beauty and awe. Stroll the 50 acres of this award-winning gem at your own pace. Learn about the 5,500 types of plants among diverse gardens, or just savor the sights and smells. Find your zen in Asian Valley, your therapy on the Woodland Walk, and your fun in the Children's Garden. Amp up your learning by taking a class—growing, drawing, or even eating plants! Schedule your visit during the annual Spring or Fall PlantFest sales or other events. In spring, take in A Million Blooms. Summertime brings Butterflies Live, Pride Month, and Flowers After 5 concerts (including dog-friendly Fidos After 5). Autumn brings splashes of color, and winter the sparkling GardenFest of Lights. Finish at the café or go to the Garden Shop for functional and decorative botanically inspired products. It's naturally delightful.

1800 Lakeside Ave., 804-262-9887
lewisginter.org

VISIT PLANTS, ANIMALS, AND THE GILDED AGE
AT MAYMONT

A wealthy Gilded Age couple cordially invites you to visit their 100-acre estate on a ridge above the James River. OK, James and Sallie May Dooley didn't invite you personally, but they willed their property to Richmond so everyone could visit. One hundred years later, the multifaceted property offers a potpourri of opportunities. Guests can take in a self-guided audio tour of the ornate mansion and servants' areas and stroll through the peaceful themed gardens and specialty habitats. Tree lovers can hug to their hearts' content at this nationally recognized arboretum, home to national and state "champion" trees. Visitors can spot local wildlife—including black bears, bald eagles, otters, and owls—pet the farm animals at the barn, and explore the area's natural history at the Robins Nature Center. Special events enhance the experience, from the Easter celebration to Summer Kickoff Concerts to fall's Garden Glow light show. Quick, RSVP "yes"!

1000 Westover Rd., 804-525-9000
maymont.org

TIP
Maymont closes during the winter, but the grounds, farm, and outdoor wildlife exhibits are open year-round.

RAISE A TOAST TO UNHAPPY HOUR
AT THE POE MUSEUM

Just what factors contributed to the dark genius of Edgar Allan Poe? How did he give life to a somber raven, a tell-tale heart, a Parisian detective, to Annabel Lee and Helen? His life, like his poems and stories, was filled with characters bitter and unkind, loving and beloved. The Poe Museum honors this 19th-century writer, who spent much of his life in Richmond. Exhibits in three historic stone buildings tell of his early years, his literary works, and his mysterious death. Artifacts and ephemera reveal lesser-known Poe trivia. Did you know that Poe pioneered sci-fi, detective stories, and horror? That a man who despised him wrote Poe's first biography? Explore the museum and sign up for the special events, like UnHappy Hour, which shed more light on his life, blending entertainment with edification. After all, the museum's goal is that Poe is underappreciated . . . nevermore.

1914 E Main St., 804-648-5523
poemuseum.org

BE INSPIRED
AT THE MAGGIE L. WALKER HOUSE

Maggie Lena Walker's story demonstrates the accomplishments of a remarkable woman and the resilience of African Americans after Emancipation. Born in Richmond in 1864, Walker received a public education, a right previously denied to Blacks. Her knowledge and passion led to a life of service, empowering Blacks and women, from Reconstruction through the early years of Jim Crow. She served as a teacher, newspaper editor, activist, fraternal leader, and the nation's first African American female bank president. The National Park Service manages the Maggie L. Walker National Historic Site, encompassing her home in historic Jackson Ward. Begin your visit with a film establishing the context of Walker's life and times. Take a guided tour of the house: see where she and her family lived; see where they entertained influential African Americans; learn what this passionate leader valued; and become inspired to use your talents to improve your own community.

600 N 2nd St., 804-226-5041, ext. 0
nps.gov/mawa

CELEBRATE RESILIENCE AND BRILLIANCE
IN JACKSON WARD

For a snapshot history of post–Civil War Black America, visit Jackson Ward, where free and newly freed Blacks built a prosperous community. Black-owned banks, including one founded by Maggie L. Walker, earned the neighborhood the title of "Black Wall Street." Venues such as the Hippodrome Theater hosted Duke Ellington and Ella Fitzgerald and other Chitlin' Circuit performers, achieving the moniker "Harlem of the South." Beginning in the 1940s, so-called urban renewal bisected the neighborhood with a new highway and destroyed homes and business. Today, the community continues to rise, stronger than ever. Visitors can visit Maggie Walker's home and statue, the Black History Museum and Cultural Center of Virginia, Elegba Folklore Society, and the Bill "Bojangles" Robinson statue. People can appreciate the historic buildings and cast-iron craftsmanship, inspiring murals, delicious food, and lively entertainment—including the 2nd Street Festival, an annual celebration of Black culture.

Black History Museum & Cultural Center of Virginia
122 W Leigh St., 804-780-9093
blackhistorymuseum.org

MOURN HISTORIC INJUSTICE AND AGONY
ON THE RICHMOND SLAVE TRAIL

From 1830 to 1860, Richmond had the ignominious distinction of being the largest source of enslaved African Americans on the East Coast. Slave ships would land at the Manchester Docks on the south bank of the James River and on Rocketts Landing on the north bank. Some enslaved people were shipped to southern ports, while others were led in coffles to auction houses around Shockoe Bottom. The Richmond Slave Trail traces the history of slavery in Richmond, beginning at the site of the Manchester Docks, over the James River, past auction houses where humans were sold and separated from families, and to Lumpkin's notorious slave jail on the Devil's Half Acre. Other notable sites on the trail include a monument to Henry Brown, who escaped in a shipping box, the Reconciliation Statue, the African Burial Ground, and First African Baptist Church. Learn from the mistakes of the past to create a better future.

The Manchester Docks, at Ancarrow's Landing
1200 Brander St., Richmond

Lumpkin's Jail
Behind Main Street Station, 1500 E Main St.
visitblkrva.com/retracing-our-past

CONTEMPLATE SOBERING TRUTHS
AT THE VIRGINIA HOLOCAUST MUSEUM

Exhibits at the Virginia Holocaust Museum add power and context to the textbook history of Nazi Germany's treatment of the Jewish people and other "undesirables." Exhibits demonstrate the abhorrent cruelty of the German regime and cooperating citizens as well as the repercussions of other nations that rejected Jewish immigrants. The museum moves beyond evil to inspiration, spotlighting tales of courage and of kindness: Jews who escaped or hid, parents who sent their children away to safe havens, non-Jews who sheltered Jews, and partisan resistance fighters. The museum highlights Richmond's Holocaust survivors, bringing history closer to home. It draws the circle of concern around other marginalized groups and shares a strong message, one vital for moving to a better future. It provides an examination of the past that's vital for understanding the present.

2000 E Cary St., 804-257-5400
vaholocaust.org

GET A CAPITAL PERSPECTIVE
ON CIVIL WAR HISTORY

As the capital of the Confederacy from 1861 to 1865, Richmond is rich with Civil War history. Begin exploring this tragic period at the American Civil War Museum, housed in historic Tredegar Iron Works, a weapons and munitions manufacturer for the South. Museum exhibits delve into the complexities of the war, showing the points of view of soldiers, families, and the enslaved. Exhibits go beyond the past, tying history to current events. The ACWM also manages the White House of the Confederacy, also known as the Confederate executive mansion. If you're still hungry for history, Richmond National Battlefield Park, part of the National Park Service, conserves 13 significant sites throughout the area, including defensive earthworks, important battlefields, trails, and Chimborazo Hospital. South of Richmond, Civil War history comes alive at Petersburg National Battlefield, Pamplin Historical Park, and Blandford Church, which boasts Louis Comfort Tiffany stained-glass windows installed to honor Southern states.

American Civil War Museum
480 Tredegar St., 804-649-1861
acwm.org

White House of the Confederacy
1201 E Clay St., 804-649-1861
acwm.org

National Battlefield Park, Richmond, Headquarters at Chimborazo Medical Museum
3215 E Broad St.
nps.gov/rich/index.htm

Petersburg National Battlefield, Eastern Front Visitor Center
5001 Siege Rd., Petersburg, 804-732-3531, ext. 200
nps.gov/pete/index.htm

Pamplin Historical Park & The National Museum of the Civil War Soldier
6125 Boydton Plank Rd., Petersburg, 877-726-7546
pamplinpark.org

Blandford Church
111 Rochelle Ln., Petersburg
bestpartva.org/do/arts-culture/blandford-church-and-cemetery

DISCOVER LIBERTY
IN CHURCH HILL AND HISTORIC ST. JOHN'S CHURCH

Taking its name from St. John's Church and from its perch atop one of Richmond's hills, Church Hill is Richmond's oldest neighborhood. Nineteenth-century homes line the streets, in a variety of architectural styles, punctuated by independent restaurants and retailers. Church Hill is home to the Chimborazo Medical Museum, educating visitors on the Civil War hospital and 1860s medicine. The neighborhood is the site of Libby Hill Park, offering a view above the James River that inspired the city's name. St. John's Church hosts the city's first public cemetery and numerous old graves, including the resting place of Eliza Poe, Edgar Allan's mother. Most notably, the church was the site of the Second Virginia Convention, March 1775, when Patrick Henry argued for revolution against the British with his fiery words, "Give me liberty, or give me death!"

Chimborazo Visitor Center and Medical Museum
3215 E Broad St.
nps.gov/rich

Historic St. John's Church
2401 E Broad St., 804-648-5015
historicstjohnschurch.org

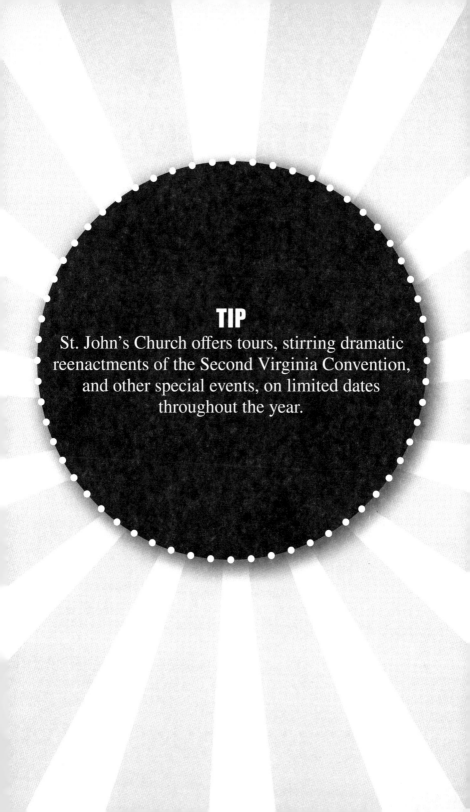

TIP

St. John's Church offers tours, stirring dramatic reenactments of the Second Virginia Convention, and other special events, on limited dates throughout the year.

GET SPOOKY
WITH HAUNTS OF RICHMOND

Beneath the dark shadows of history lurk restless spirits who sneak out to wander among us. Their stories tell tales of love and loss, hate and cruelty, social despair and political unrest. Knowledgeable tour guides from Haunts of Richmond expound upon these tales, from spectral children playing at the Poe Museum, spirits that tease the Capitol Police, a sorrowful soldier who still guards the Masons' Hall, and a ghostly woman who mourns at the site of the Church Hill train tunnel collapse. Haunts of Richmond's guides illuminate the city's history through spooky legends, drawn from historical research and firsthand experiences. Tour groups stroll the city's old neighborhoods, including Shockoe, Church Hill, Capitol Hill, Franklin Street, Court End—and even VCU. Dogs are welcome, too—possibly perceptive of wandering spirits. Guests are regaled with mournful and spine-tingling tales as the chill of the unknown blows past— whatever the season.

804-543-3189
hauntsofrichmond.com

CELEBRATE THE LIFE OF A RICHMOND GOAT
AT THE ARTHUR ASHE MONUMENT

The monument to Arthur Ashe celebrates the native Richmonder who gained worldwide recognition as a professional tennis player. He became the first African American to win the US Open in 1968, the Australian Open in 1970, and Wimbledon in 1975; he was also an educator, humanitarian, and Civil Rights activist. The monument reflects the progress of Blacks in Richmond. While Ashe's early years were marred by segregation, by exclusion from Whites-only tennis courts and tournaments, the city eventually recognized his contributions. Richmond named an athletic center for him in 1982, erected the monument in 1996, and renamed a street for him in 2019. The statue portrays Ashe surrounded by children, a tennis racket in one hand and books in the other, reflecting his emphasis on the sport and education.

At the intersection of Monument Avenue and Roseneath Road

SALUTE THE DEAD AND THE VIEWS
AT HOLLYWOOD CEMETERY

It's a cemetery! It's a park! It's both! Hollywood Cemetery is a peaceful resting place for the dead and a fascinating, scenic landscape for the living. Established atop the banks of the James River in 1847, the 135-acre garden cemetery hosts an array of distinctive memorials situated on sharply rolling hills, punctuated by stately native trees. Highlights include the graves of US presidents James Monroe and John Tyler, Civil War Confederate president Jefferson Davis, Supreme Court justice Lewis Powell, authors Ellen Glasgow and Tom Wolfe, and GWAR musician and artist Dave Brockie. Look for the 90-foot-tall pyramidal monument to Confederate casualties, the legendary cast-iron Newfoundland dog, an array of fascinating grave markers, Instagrammable views of the James River and Richmond's skyline—and maybe some spooky apparitions!

412 S Cherry St., 804-648-8501
hollywoodcemetery.org

TIP

Get the most out of your visit with a tour. Options are noted on Hollywood Cemetery's website, from self-guided maps to professional tours during warm months, such as Valentine walking tours and by Segway, trolley, and electric Tuk Tuk.

SEE HOW ART BEAUTIFIES AND INSPIRES
WITH RICHMOND'S MURALS

Richmond's public art has taken off since artist Mickael Broth was arrested in 2004 for artistic graffiti. Since then, others have joined in legally painting the town red, including well-known artists like Hamilton Glass, Ed Trask, Nils Westergard, Emily Herr, and Matt Lively. More than 150 murals adorn buildings throughout the city, a rotating exhibit of creativity, wacky, whimsical, and meaningful. Picture a levitating segmented woman, a cartoon rabbit in motion, enamored astronauts, and bees on cycles. The Mending Walls RVA project has added more meaning to Richmond's public art, pairing artists of different backgrounds to create murals highlighting social injustice. *Together We Rise*, for example, mimics faded ads on historic Richmond buildings. In the foreground, a Black woman and a White woman, wrapped with barricade tape imprinted with victims' names, help each other stand. Behind the women are three social mantras, set in old ad fonts. "We need to talk," the Mending Walls project states. Murals spark the conversation.

Mending Walls RVA
mendingwallsrva.com/map

Richmond Mural Project
richmondmuralproject.squarespace.com

TIP

For richer context, view *Mending Walls: The Documentary*. A link to the PBS documentary is available at mendingwallsrva.com or pbs.org.

TRAVEL 400 YEARS BACK IN TIME
AT HENRICUS HISTORICAL PARK

At this outdoor living history museum, costumed interpreters and re-created buildings shed light on the life of 17th-century Virginia settlers and Indigenous people. Established by Sir Thomas Dale in 1611, the "citie" saw early cultivation of tobacco, that game-changing cash crop, as well as the first English hospital and college in the New World. The settlement also hosted the Indian princess Pocahontas, who lived there after her capture. A period house, tavern, tobacco barn, blacksmith's forge, and other structures illustrate life in the colony. An Arrohateck Indian village shows the life of the people who lived here before the settlers. The bluff above the James River tells other snippets of history, including a canal constructed by the US Colored Troops during the Civil War and John Smith's meeting with the Arrohateck. For the complete experience, time your visit to catch one of the park's special events.

251 Henricus Park Rd., Chester, 804-748-1611
henricus.org

HAVE A BALL WITH STEM
AT THE SCIENCE MUSEUM OF VIRGINIA

After pondering the 29-ton granite globe in front of the museum, move inside to play with—aka learn about—the mysteries of reality. Proclaiming that the word "museum" is a verb, the Science Museum of Virginia packs its galleries with entertaining hands-on activities. Play games that challenge the mind and the body, like air hockey against a computer or a pitching cage and a sprint measuring speed. Feel the power of hurricane-force winds. Be inspired by scientists and mind-blowing ideas. Get creative in workshops combining art and science. Surround yourself with wonders at The Dome, one of the world's most technologically advanced theaters. Youthful inquiring minds, from toddlers on up, can get involved in galleries designed just for them. Whatever your age, roll up your sleeves and get engaged while learning science, technology, engineering, and math. You'll have a world of fun and gain a universe of memories.

2500 W Broad St., 804-864-1400
smv.org

TIP
Consult the calendar to get the most out of your visit, including Dome shows, special and recurring events, live demos, and traveling exhibitions. The museum resides in and around a historic 223,000-square-foot train station, so look for mementoes of the past throughout the museum as well the Model Railroad Show in December.

PAY YOUR RESPECTS
AT THE VIRGINIA WAR MEMORIAL

Dignity, honor, appreciation, and light—the Virginia War Memorial honors the fallen soldiers who called the Commonwealth home. Perched nobly on a hill near Richmond's downtown, the memorial provides expansive views of the skyline and the river—as if seeing into the distance of ever-changing time. The structure began with one grand Shrine of Memory, dedicated in 1956. At the Shrine, a sculpture of a grieving woman stands beside a glass wall with the names and hometowns of casualties from World War II and the Korean War. A new wall was added for Virginians killed in action in subsequent wars, including Vietnam, Gulf Wars, and other 21st-century conflicts. The memorial has expanded to include meaningful permanent and changing exhibits, services, and programs, educating the public while saluting the valor of Virginians who have served our nation.

621 S Belvidere St., 804-786-2060
vawarmemorial.org

GET ARTSY
WITH FIRST FRIDAY ART WALKS

The Richmond Arts District throws a party on the first Friday of every month—and you're invited! Art galleries, creative retailers, and restaurants all get involved. First Fridays showcase ever-changing exhibits, with chances to chat with artists at some of the city's best galleries and studios, including the Institute for Contemporary Arts at Virginia Commonwealth University. Wandering guests can attend opening exhibits and catch amazing live performances, from groundbreaking music to belly-busting comedy, and then stop at a nearby restaurant or bar for sustenance. First Fridays offer the chance to feel the creative vibe of Richmond's art scene and reflect on the city's energy, diversity, and cultural renaissance. Constraint is anathema to creativity, so galleries grace other parts of the city, too— approximately 70 galleries call the Richmond region home.

facebook.com/rvafirstfridays

TIP
Check the First Fridays Facebook page for updated information and cover charges (when applicable) as well as parking and public transportation options.

GET DERAILED
AT THE RICHMOND RAILROAD MUSEUM

There's something appealing about the power of trains. Richmond has been served by multiple railroads since the 1830s, and it continues to use freight and Amtrak passenger service. Richmond's triple crossing bridge, possibly the only place where three railroads cross at a single point, is part of a three-mile long, double-track viaduct. The iconic 1919 railroad bridge west of the city was constructed with large and small arches, resembling a Roman aqueduct. Repurposed train stations still stand proud, including Main Street Station in Shockoe Bottom, Broad Street Station (now the Science Museum of Virginia), and the SR Station on Hull Street, which is now the Richmond Railroad Museum. The museum offers the chance to learn more about railroad history in Richmond and beyond, to enjoy a room filled with model railroads chugging through settings inspired by Richmond and Virginia, and to climb aboard a caboose.

102 Hull St., 804-231-4324
richmondrailroadmuseum.com

SEE WHERE WHEELS OF POWER TURN
AT THE VIRGINIA STATE CAPITOL AND CAPITOL SQUARE

What do you get when you combine centuries of history with history in the making? Virginia's state capitol building! The Richmond capitol building, designed by Thomas Jefferson, was constructed for the Virginia legislature, which has been meeting there since 1788. A 21st-century expansion went underground, adding space without detracting from the grandeur of the original. A tour of the capitol building captures history, architecture, and art. Highlights include the dramatic rotunda, topped by a skylit dome and marked with an original statue of George Washington and busts of the seven other Virginians who became US presidents. Capitol Square, surrounding the capitol and the Governor's Mansion, hosts multiple monuments in 12 parklike acres, including the Virginia Civil Rights Memorial centered on Barbara Johns, a young woman who stood for equal education; the Virginia Women's Monument, 11 influential Virginia women; the George Washington Equestrian Monument to Revolutionary patriots; and the Mantle, a tribute to Virginia's indigenous tribes.

1000 Bank St., 804-698-1788
virginiacapitol.gov

Mongrel in Carytown
Credit: Sarah Ann Atkins/Virginia Tourism Corporation

SHOPPING
AND FASHION

SHOP THE MILE OF STYLE
IN CARYTOWN

The story of this consumer paradise began with Cary Court Park & Shop in 1938, the city's first "shopping center." Since then, the district has spread up and down Cary Street to encompass a "Mile of Style," nurturing some of Richmond's long-time favorite businesses. Dozens of independent retailers, restaurants, services, and entertainment businesses line the sidewalks, appealing to shoppers of all ages and backgrounds. Find stylish clothing, jewelry, and accessories. Hunt for unique, hilarious, and luxurious gifts and stationery. Shop games, sporting goods, organic groceries, home décor, and more. Between shopping the shops, treat yourself to an array of foods: French, Thai, and Indian cuisine; sweets; craft beer; cocktails; pizza; and deli delights. Carytown also hosts popular annual events, such as the August Carytown Watermelon Festival and October Zombie Walk.

TIP
The district offers street parking along Cary Street and several parking lots. If you don't find parking on Cary, the nearby residential streets are open to public parking.

For the Love of Chocolate
Thousands of cocoa and candy confections
from all over the world
3136 W Cary St., 804-359-5645
fortheloveofchocolaterva.com

Lex's of Carytown
Outfitting women for special occasions—proms, weddings,
and other formal events—in a variety of styles and sizes
3018 W Cary St., 804-355-5425
lexsofcarytown.com

Pop of Confetti
Twenty-plus women-owned businesses that curate
and create whimsical and thoughtful accessories,
jewelry, stationery, and gifts
3422 W Cary St., 804-294-0050
popofconfetti.com

Traveling Chic Boutique
The latest fashions in clothing, shoes, intimate apparel,
and more, with limited quantities of each style to
ensure unique looks
3143 W Cary St., 804-837-4027
shoptcbrichmond.com

World of Mirth
Toys, games, and laughs for kids of all ages—really!
3005 W Cary St., 804-353-8991
worldofmirth.com

FEAST AND FEST ON VIRGINIA FRESH
AT THE RVA BIG MARKET

Picture 100 vendors—farmers, bakers, chefs, crafters, and more—all gathered in one peaceful, verdant park. Independent vendors are hawking produce, eggs, meats, freshly prepared foods, and a multitude of other goods. Better yet, at this producer-only market, all products for sale must be homegrown or homemade in Virginia, by the vendor. This visualization becomes reality every Saturday morning at the RVA Big Market in Bryan Park, in Richmond's Northside, conveniently just off I-95. Are you in search of delicious fresh produce, eggs, meats, sausage, or cheese? Hungry for a hot brunch, cold ice cream, piping hot coffee, fresh pastries, or healthy juices, kefir, and kombucha? Searching for crafted gifts, souvenirs, or home goods such as candles, woodworks, jewelry, pottery, and prints—including some that celebrate life in Richmond? You'll find it here! And if you visit during springtime azalea season, you'll find yourself surrounded by hosts of colorful blooms.

Hosted by Grow RVA at Bryan Park, 4308 Hermitage Rd.
growrva.com/rvabigmkt

TIP

Wear comfortable walking shoes and arrive early—8 a.m. or soon after in the summer, 9 a.m. or soon after for the winter market. Crowds grow as the morning wears on, and the market closes promptly at noon.

GIVE A GIFT OF RICHMOND
AT THE VALENTINE MUSEUM SHOP

Products made in Richmond and those celebrating the city make appearances in many shops around town. Besides hand-crafted swag and informative books, keep your eyes peeled for incredible foods, like AR's Hot Southern Honey, Mother Shrub drinking vinegar, Jonesin' for a Treat healthy dog biscuits, Back Pocket Provisions Bloody Mary mixes, and decadent Nightingale ice cream sandwiches. You'll find these distinctive products in independent markets, boutique shops, and museum stores. Possibly the best place to find locally made products and quality branded swag is the small-but-mighty Valentine Museum gift shop. The shop complements the museum's Richmond focus by offering a rich selection of Richmond goods, from food and kitchen linens to books and only-in-RVA clothing, kitchenware, and accessories. The shop also offers limited releases of Valentine's Meat Juice Bloody Mary Mix, a tasty concoction with a colorful Richmond backstory. The original Meat Juice, created in 1870 by Mann Valentine for his ailing wife, ultimately lined his pockets with wealth.

1015 E Clay St., 804-649-0711
thevalentine.org

OUTFIT
YOUR BODY AND SOUL
AT ALTERNATIVES BOUTIQUE

Chances are, you buy clothes that make you feel good. The material feels nice on the skin, it fits comfortably, and it makes you feel like a million bucks. Clothing at AlterNatives Boutique does all that and more. Like the moonlight blue scarf made of soft Alpaca fleece, created by and supporting an indigenous producer—the scarf is soft and eye-catching, and you can smile knowing you've helped a talented artisan. Or warm your wardrobe and your heart with a striped linen dress, embroidered top, crinkle-cotton gauze blouse, lace palazzo pants, or sleeveless crocheted top. AlterNatives, an indigenous, woman-owned business and social enterprise, sources these and other fair trade products, providing indigenous producers with the opportunity to provide for their families and communities. So shop AlterNatives and feel good through and through.

3320 W Cary St., 804-342-5886
alternatives.boutique

GET A TATTOO
IN RVA

Got ink? Want ink? Richmond has you covered! RVA has been ranked third among tattoo-friendly American cities, with more than 14 tattoo shops per 100k people and plenty of ink on the streets and in workplaces. The region even hosts the world's longest-running tattoo convention each fall. The diversity of artists and styles makes it a great place to start or add to a skin-art collection. One studio, Loose Screw Tattoo, was founded in 2011 by internationally known, professionally trained artist Jesse Smith. The shop features a dozen skilled artists and hosts guest tattoo artists from around the world. Importantly, Loose Screw Tattoo also commits to rigorous cleaning and sterilization procedures for all its artists and stations. Loose Screw and other Richmond studios practically guarantee that time spent in Richmond can make you more appealing than ever!

3313-A W Cary St., 804-342-1981
loosescrewtattoo.com

TIP

Most tattoo studios are by appointment only, so be sure to reach out ahead of time. You can explore artists' styles on their websites and Instagram feeds.

Black Rabbit Tattoo
Woman-run studio that celebrates diversity
and authenticity and hosts guest artists
17 N Belmont Ave., 804-353-1002
instagram.com/black_rabbit_tattoo

Salvation Tattoo Gallery
More than a half-dozen artists specializing
in a diversity of styles
819 W Cary St., 804-643-3779
salvationgallery.com

Heroes & Ghosts Tattoo
Offers piercings as well as tattoos
3035 W Cary St., 804-342-0042
heroesandghoststattoo.com

Amy Black Tattoos
Specializes in custom tattoos and mastectomy tattooing
3125 W Cary St., 2nd fl., 804-254-9006
amyblacktattoos.com

Richmond Tattoo Art & Music Festival
Dozens of tattoo artists ply their trade, accompanied
by musical acts and merchandise vendors
richmondtattooconvention.com

SHOP THE PAST FOR CLASSIC STYLES
AT BYGONES VINTAGE

Whether you're repurposing clothing to benefit the Earth, outfitting yourself in coastal grandmother style, looking for a unique gift, or shopping for distinctive clothing to spark your wardrobe, Richmond's vintage clothing stores have you covered. Not even counting Goodwill stores scattered around the region, Richmond is home to a host of secondhand stores that specialize in quality used clothing, jewelry, and accessories. The premiere Richmond vintage store, Bygones Vintage, has been outfitting style-conscious men and women for more than 40 years. Most notably stocked with items from the early 1900s to the groovy year of 1969, the store sells classic clothing and accessories from head to toe. Bygones also stocks a splash of fabulous new items, to help ensure a completely coordinated look (crocheted head scarves, sequins, or Pyknic foodie clothing, anyone?). Nostalgia is welcome, but it's entirely optional!

2916 W Cary St., 804-353-1919
bygonesvintage.com

FIND DOWN-HOME FRIENDLY ALONGSIDE GLOBAL INFLUENCES
AT SHAKOOR'S MERCHANDISE

Shakoor's Merchandise packs an abundance of goodness in a small space. For more than 20 years, the family-owned business has been serving the historic Jackson Ward neighborhood, both with its inventory and as a safe space for the community. The patriarch began as a street vendor before opening the storefront in 2002, with a modest space appealing to diverse niche markets. Apparel displayed proudly along one wall highlights mostly Afro-centric garments, as well as prayer rugs and other textiles. Besides the colorful, eye-catching clothing, you'll find a host of other products with broad appeal: natural soaps, teas, health tonics, jewelry, incense, frozen Ali bean pies, and an array of exotic and essential body oils. Don't miss those body oils—the friendly staff will help you find a favorite scent to enhance your person or your space—personalized aromatherapy!

319 N 2nd St., 804-644-4494
shakoorsmerchandise.com

BRING YOUR PERFECT ART HOME
FROM CROSSROADS ART CENTER

Wander the colorful, sprawling maze of galleries at Crossroads Art Center, past oodles of art lining walls, windows, and stalls. Feast your eyes and soul on the creations of 225 emerging and established mid-Atlantic artists. Take in the rich variety of media: glass, mosaics, paintings, photography, pottery, sculpture, metalwork, wood, jewelry, and textiles. Stroll the galleries simply for inspiration, to appreciate the talent and breathtaking beauty, or to look for art that beckons you to take it home. Given the range of price points, you'll want to be on the lookout for unique gifts, too. Because of the focus on local artists, you'll find an abundance of local landmarks celebrating the region through art. For a more immersive experience, attend Crossroads' special exhibitions, events, juried shows, and classes. Check out the online shop, too, for a preview of the art or to shop from home.

2016 Staples Mill Rd., 804-278-8950
crossroadsartcenter.com

DELIGHT IN DIVERSE SHOPPING
AT THE SHOPS AT 5807

Are you in search of distinctive, whimsical, functional, or eye-catching décor, clothing, and accessories? Entertaining toys or cute kids' clothing? Stationery that makes a statement or special gifts that show you care? You'll find all that and more at The Shops at 5807, an "eclectic small-mall." Each of the two dozen vendors has carefully curated its collection, learning what shoppers want and perfecting its inventory accordingly. Think neon pink insulated "Margatini" tumblers, elegant napkin rings, nostalgic toys, pimento cheese popcorn, statement scarves, golf cart earrings, ruffled skirts, designer poop-bag pouches—then multiply those items by the hundreds and you'll get the picture! With all the careful curation, you're bound to find plenty to please your shopping bag, your pocketbook, and everyone on your gift list.

5807 Patterson Ave., 804-288-5807
shop5807.com

START YOUR TROPICAL ORCHID COLLECTION
AT CHADWICK & SON ORCHIDS

The father-and-son team of A. A. Chadwick and Arthur E. Chadwick wrote the book on orchids—*The Classic Cattleyas*—then they wrote another one—*First Ladies and Their Cattleyas: A Century of Namesake Orchids*. Art Sr. began growing these elegant plants in 1945. In 1989, he, his wife, and their son opened Chadwick & Son Orchids retail shop and greenhouse in Powhatan County, just west of Richmond. The staff's devotion and knowledge results in vigorous, healthy, and delicately beautiful orchids—cattleyas, phalaenopsis, slipper orchids, and more—to grace your home or office. The business now has 11 greenhouses and three retail stores. Chadwick also offers a "boarding" service to flower-sit your orchid, after the flower fades and the plant goes droopy and dormant. Then, when you fetch it, it's blooming and thriving and beautiful again!

1240 Dorset Rd., Powhatan, 804-598-7560
203 N Belmont Ave., 804-359-6724
1125 Gaskins Rd., Henrico, 804-709-1133
chadwickorchids.com

TIP

All three locations sell orchids and arrange for boarding, but at the Powhatan greenhouses, you can wander through the rows of orchids, on your own or in a guided tour.

"MEAT" YOUR NEXT GREAT HOME-COOKED MEAL
AT BELMONT BUTCHERY

The sign above the meat counter at Belmont Butchery proudly proclaims its philosophy: "Being vegetarian is a big missed steak." Owner Tanya Cauthen has been sharpening her craft for decades, appreciating meat and respecting the animals that provide it. She opened her butcher shop in 2006, inspired not just to prepare fine cuts of meat, nose to tail, but especially to share expertise with Richmond's consumers. She gained national attention on Food Network's *Chopped* and in prestigious food-focused magazines. The butchery sources from carefully chosen farms, stocking beef, pork, chicken, lamb, house-made sausages, bacon, charcuterie, exotic meats, unexpected cuts, and more. Belmont Butchery also sells products to enhance your meaty dinner, including cheeses, sauces, sides, and wines. But best of all, the butchery offers expert advice—at no extra charge!

15 N Belmont Ave., 804-422-8519
belmontbutchery.com

FIND YOUR GROOVE
AT PLAN 9 MUSIC

More than 40 years of experience as an independent music store gives Plan 9 added respect for audio recording media and musicians across the decades. The store carries new and used LPs, CDs, and cassettes as well as stereo equipment. It specializes in a wide selection of premium and affordable used vinyl, including 45s, 78s, and LPs. You'll find music across genres, from rock and pop to funk and jazz, world music, classical, blues, and more. Plan 9 and Richmond's music scene enjoy a symbiotic relationship. The store carries hundreds of titles on consignment from area bands, offers in-store performances and release parties, and supports the annual Richmond Folk Festival. And since employees are music fans themselves, they can help guide customers in expanding their collections and horizons. Find more of what you already love, or find some new notes to admire!

3017 W Cary St., 804-353-9996
plan9music.com

BE DOGGED IN YOUR SEARCH FOR CURIOUS GIFTS
AT MONGREL

Mongrel (noun): a dog of unknown breed or type. While the word for a beloved pet can be considered an insult, this eclectic retailer embraces it proudly. Mongrel's products range from decorative, useful, and sentimental to irreverent and unapologetically woke. In two deep rooms packed with merchandise, the store sells stylish home décor, quirky but useful kitchen goods, scented candles, unexpected cookbooks, and stationery. The store carries a selection of Richmond-branded products and books, including Mongrel exclusives. Mongrel is perhaps best known for products that generate lots of laughs and huzzahs of the PG-13 ilk: drinking games, suggestive greeting cards, political humor, bawdy magnets, novelty socks, and products celebrating pride and feminism. Unique, unexpected, and hilarious—Mongrel has been recognized in RVA as its own breed of store since 1991.

2924 W Cary St., 804-342-1272
mongrelrva.com

BRING YOUR HOME INTO THE MODERN WORLD
AT LADIFF

Creative contemporary furniture at this classic Richmond store seems to transport you to the future. While many furniture stores tip their hats to classic styles, LaDiff has chosen a different focus since 1980. Working with many suppliers through the years, including international suppliers from Scandinavia, Italy, and elsewhere, the business has found the best of the best and built strong relationships that ensure quality and service. Besides being wildly stylish, pieces can be amazingly comfortable and refreshingly kid friendly—like ergonomic office chairs and kid-proof textiles. At LaDiff, customers work with design consultants to outfit every room of their house as well as their outdoor spaces. While furniture establishes the foundation, accessories set the mood—the perfect lighting, rugs, and accents. At this local Richmond store, distinctive European styles can help set your home apart. Vive la différence!

1011 Commerce Rd., 866-452-3433
ladiff.com

FIND NEW OLD DÉCOR
AT CARAVATI'S
ARCHITECTURAL SALVAGE

Old is the name of the game at Caravati's. The business is old, started by Louis Caravati in 1939. It operates out of an old Ford dealership and it gives new life to old products. An architectural salvage company, Caravati's sells materials and fixtures from buildings being demolished or renovated and gives them new life elsewhere. Think woodwork, doorways and doors, bathroom fixtures, doorknobs, fireplace mantels, counters, flooring, stonework, and more. The showroom also repurposes pieces large and small—like a section of bowling alley floor as a tabletop and dried flowers in doorknob "vases." These aged materials can enhance your home or business, adding vintage touches, unique adornments, and artistic flourishes. The business began in Richmond's Manchester neighborhood and moved to Ashland in 2022, but it's still family owned and operated. Some old things just continue going strong!

201 England St., Ashland, 804-232-4175
caravatis.com

CATCH GOOD VIBES
AT ALCHEMISTS

In centuries past, alchemy sought to transform metals into gold and discover the elixir for eternal life. While those goals were never achieved, alchemists did discover distillation and supported transcendent philosophies. At Alchemists in Richmond, "alchemy" is a metaphor for transformation, transforming consciousness from mundane to spiritual. The store is a peaceful oasis in a welcoming atmosphere, offering books, classes, readings, and special events for spiritual development and comfort. Artisan-made jewelry and other products provide beauty that soothes the soul. Candles, crystals, sound healing tools, stones, incense, and sage—along with classes such as tarot, crystals, and shamanism—take healing to the next level. Even if you don't embrace the spiritual principles at Alchemists, the products make wonderful gifts for yourself or someone else, like soothing windchimes, enriching home décor, and delightfully scented products, all bringing joy and pleasure. Alchemists is an oasis of peace and relaxation for the body, mind, and spirit.

3080 Stony Point Rd., 804-320-9200
alchemistsrva.com

TRAIN YOUR SIGHTS ON SMALL-TOWN CHARM
IN ASHLAND

Homespun atmosphere and railroad lore weave through Ashland. The town began as a resort and a stop along the RF&P Railroad. Incorporated in 1858, it became home to Randolph-Macon College in 1868. The railroad and college helped keep Ashland strong, and the town's residents have kept it vibrant. Shops and restaurants along Railroad Avenue, on both sides of the track, have front-row views of passing trains (more than 60 per day), accompanied by the trains' whistles, powerful engines, and percussive sounds of the wheels. Ashland, fondly dubbed "The Center of the Universe," hosts annual events such as Light Up the Tracks and Ashland Train Days. The renovated Ashland Theatre feeds fun with movies and entertainment, while restaurants and a brewery feed the body and unique independent retailers feed the shopping bug.

ashlandvirginia.com

TIP

For the full railroad experience, linger along Railroad Street to catch a passing train, marvel at artist Ed Trask's bigger-than-life train mural (108 S Railroad St.), stop by the 1923 train depot (across from the Henry Clay Inn), and climb aboard the caboose at the Ashland Museum.

Tiny Tim's Toys & Trains
Model trains and a variety of toys, for fun, creativity, and education, including for special needs children
104 S Railroad Ave., Ashland, 804-368-0063
trainandtoystore.com

Changing Reins
Gently used horse-riding equipment and apparel, plus home décor, clothing, and jewelry for horse lovers
102 S Railroad Ave., Ashland, 804-752-6782
changingreinsinc.com

Thrill of the Hunt
Stylish upcycled and new furniture, home décor, custom lighting, local art, vintage products, and DIY Annie Sloan paint products and workshops
315 England St., Ashland, 804-368-0184
thrillofthehuntva.com

Ashland Meat Company @ Cross Brothers
Quality, humanely raised meats and an on-site butcher plus a curated selection of local provisions
107 S Railroad St., Ashland, 804-798-8311
ashlandmeatco.com

The Caboose Market and Café
Food, wine, beer, cheese, Virginia products, and house-made foods, enjoyed in the café or toted home from the market
108 S Railroad Ave., Ashland, 804-798-2933
cabooseashland.com

Center of the Yarniverse
The center of heaven for knitters, with yarns in a variety of fibers and textures, to knit and crochet, plus patterns, kits, accessories, and classes
100 N Railroad Ave., Ashland, 804-362-7800
centeroftheyarniverse.com

TURN OVER A NEW LEAF
AT INDEPENDENT BOOKSTORES

The struggles of independent bookstores got a humorous romantic treatment in 1998's *You've Got Mail*—book lovers ached for Meg Ryan and continued to frequent local businesses. Richmond's local bookstores make supporting them easy, offering services such as special orders, out-of-print book searches, used books, and personalized service. Fountain Bookstore has been nurturing bibliophiles and authors since 1978. Located in historic Shockoe Bottom, the store provides customers with a steady stream of new books, thematic book clubs, recommendations, and autographed copies, available at the store and online for shipping worldwide. Fountain Bookstore also offers free, diverse, and creative author programming, bringing in local, regional, and nationally known personalities. In addition to in-store and virtual programs and signings, the store partners with the community to host author programs at local venues, including historic landmarks, an art studio, and libraries.

1312 E Cary St., 804-788-1594
fountainbookstore.com

BBGB Tales for Kids
Mostly kids' books, with a focus on titles that inspire
and open readers' minds to the world
3003 W Cary St., 804-353-5675
bbgbbooks.com

Book People
New and used fiction and nonfiction titles, a foreign language
section, special orders, out-of-print book search,
and puzzles and games
10464 Ridgefield Pkwy., Henrico, 804-288-4346
bookpeoplerichmond.com

Shelf Life Books
A large selection of new books on the
main level and used books upstairs
2913 W Cary St., 804-422-8066
shelflifebooksrva.com

The Book Bar
A Black-owned, woman-owned store that centers BIPOC
authors and brands, plus a wine bar, special events,
book club, and quarterly subscription boxes
1311 E Main St.
rvabookbar.com

The Little Bookshop
Offers books, book clubs, and author events
to the Midlothian community
1318 Sycamore Sq., Midlothian, 804-464-1244
thelittlebookshopva.com

Virginia Shop at the Library of Virginia
A shop full of Virginia-focused books and gifts, plus library-
hosted virtual book clubs, author talks, and literary awards
800 E Broad St., 804-692-3524
thevirginiashop.org

ACTIVITIES
BY SEASON

SPRING

Run with a Gang . . . of Runners with Sports Backers and RRRC, 70
See Why It's All Greek to Us at Stella's, 2
Party at Richmond's Longest-Running Concert Series, Friday Cheers, 55
Chill Out, Work Out, or Rock Out at Dominion Riverrock, 68
Cruise the Virginia Capital Trail, 64
Explore a Bounty of Flowers and Fun at Lewis Ginter Botanical Garden, 85

SUMMER

"Have Funn and Go Nuts" with the Flying Squirrels, 61
Get Carried Away on the James River with Riverside Outfitters, 73
Shop the Mile of Style in Carytown, 110
Discover Liberty in Church Hill and Historic St. John's Church, 94
Get a Kick Out of the Richmond Kickers, 63
Immerse Yourself in Richmond's History with the Valentine, 82
Feast and Fest on Virginia Fresh at the RVA Big Market, 112
Follow the Richmond Beer Trail, 15

FALL

Run with a Gang . . . of Runners with Sports Backers and RRRC, 70

Surround Yourself with World Culture at the Richmond Folk Festival, 40

Visit Plants, Animals, and the Gilded Age at Maymont, 86

Wine Down on the Banks of the James at Upper Shirley Vineyards, 23

Get Spooky with Haunts of Richmond, 96

Salute the Dead and the Views at Hollywood Cemetery, 98

Raise a Toast to UnHappy Hour at the Poe Museum, 87

WINTER

Get in the Spirit with Craft Distilleries, 20

Get in the Christmas Spirit with Richmond's Holiday Lights, 52

Celebrate Resilience and Brilliance in Jackson Ward, 89

Have a Wild, Aww-Mazing Time at the Metro Richmond Zoo, 46

Be Entertained at Ornate Historic Venues, 44

SUGGESTED ITINERARIES

HAVE A DAY WITH THE DOGS

Treat Your Dog to a Romp at Ruff Canine Club, 77

Traverse the Trails of the James River Park System, 60

Find a Park Lover's Paradise at Pocahontas State Park, 62

Follow the Richmond Beer Trail, 15

"Have Funn and Go Nuts" with the Flying Squirrels, 61

Get a Kick Out of the Richmond Kickers, 63

Explore a Bounty of Flowers and Fun at Lewis Ginter Botanical Garden, 85

CRAFT BEVERAGES

Don't Worry, Be Hoppy with Hazy Richmond IPAs, 16

See What the Buzz Is About with Mead and Cider, 18

Savor a Perfect Pairing, 24

Follow the Richmond Beer Trail, 15

Get in the Spirit with Craft Distilleries, 20

Wine Down on the Banks of the James at Upper Shirley Vineyards, 23

Find Your Cheers at The Jasper, 26

Try the Threesome of Beer, Burgers, and Adult Shakes at Station 2, 27

COSMOPOLITAN VIBES

Surround Yourself with World Culture at the Richmond Folk Festival, 40

Find the Answer to RVA Beer and Vietnamese Fare at Mekong and The Answer, 14

Find Down-Home Friendly alongside Global Influences at Shakoor's Merchandise, 119

Outfit Your Body and Soul at AlterNatives Boutique, 115

Marvel at Worldwide Creativity, Thoughtfulness, and Beauty at the VMFA, 84

Outfit Your House at LaDiff, 127

Be Part of a 2,000-Year-Old Tradition at the Richmond International Dragon Boat Festival, 76

Catch a Classic at the Classic Byrd Theatre, 34

• •

OLD RICHMOND

Immerse Yourself in Richmond's History with the Valentine, 82

Get a Taste of Richmond's History at Ukrop's Market Hall, 6

Get Boxed In with a Smile at Sally Bell's Kitchen, 3

Dine in History at the Jefferson, 10

Catch a Classic at the Classic Byrd Theatre, 34

Discover Liberty in Church Hill and Historic St. John's Church, 94

Get Swept Up in the Drama at a Local Theater, 42

Visit Plants, Animals, and the Gilded Age at Maymont, 86

Shop the Mile of Style in Carytown, 110

Salute the Dead and the Views at Hollywood Cemetery, 98

FOODIE FAVORITES

Worship High Cuisine on Church Hill, 5

Elevate Your Dining at L'Opossum, 4

See Why It's All Greek to Us at Stella's, 2

Conjure a Beloved Italian Grandmother at Edo's Squid, 29

Spoil Your Sweet Tooth at Shyndigz, 8

Appreciate the Evolution of BBQ at ZZQ, 25

TRAVEL BACK IN TIME

Travel 400 Years Back in Time at Henricus Historical Park, 102

Get Spooky with Haunts of Richmond, 96

Raise a Toast to UnHappy Hour at the Poe Museum, 87

Visit Plants, Animals, and the Gilded Age at Maymont, 86

Mourn Historic Injustice and Agony on the Richmond Slave Trail, 90

Be Inspired at the Maggie L. Walker House, 88

Contemplate Sobering Truths at the Virginia Holocaust Museum, 91

Immerse Yourself in Richmond's History with the Valentine, 82

Traverse Four Unique Trails along the James, 66

Engage with History at the Virginia Museum of History & Culture, 83

FAMILY-FRIENDLY

Visit Plants, Animals, and the Gilded Age at Maymont, 86

Take a Child to Play and Learn to Love at PARK365, 75

Learn through Fun at the Children's Museum of Richmond, 45

Have a Ball with STEM at the Science Museum of Virginia, 103

Engage with History at the Virginia Museum of History & Culture, 83

Have a Wild, Aww-Mazing Time at the Metro Richmond Zoo, 46

GET YOUR HEART PUMPING

Cruise the Virginia Capital Trail, 64

Traverse the Trails of the James River Park System, 60

Chill Out, Work Out, or Rock Out at Dominion Riverrock, 68

Find a Park Lover's Paradise at Pocahontas State Park, 62

Climb the Wall at the Old Manchester Bridge, 74

Get Carried Away on the James River with Riverside Outfitters, 73

HAVE A MEMORABLE DATE NIGHT

Elevate Your Dining at L'Opossum, 4

Get Swept Up in the Drama at a Local Theater, 42

Roll Up Your Sleeves at a Cooking Class, 22

Wine Down on the Banks of the James at Upper Shirley Vineyards, 23

Laugh until You Cry at Local Comedy Venues, 36

Dance like You're in the Tropics at Havana '59, 51

Have a One-Stop Night Out at The Tin Pan, 38

BE PART OF RICHMOND'S DIVERSITY

Celebrate Resilience and Brilliance in Jackson Ward, 89

Celebrate Fabulous Diversity at Godfrey's Drag Brunch, 53

Catch the Soul of the City, 30

See Where Wheels of Power Turn at the Virginia State Capitol and Capitol Square, 107

Take a Child to Play and Learn to Love at PARK365, 75

Find a Park Lover's Paradise at Pocahontas State Park, 62

• •

INDEX

2nd Street Festival, 89

Adventures in RVA, 65

Alchemists, 129

Alewife, 5

AlterNatives Boutique, 115

Altria Theater, 44

American Civil War Museum, 92–93

Amy Black Tattoos, 117

Ancarrow's Landing, 60, 90

Answer Brewpub, The, 14

Ardent Craft Ales, 15

AR's Hot Southern Honey, 114

Arthur Ashe Monument, 97

Ashland, 72, 128, 130–131

Ashland Meat Company @ Cross Brothers, 131

Ashland Museum, 130

Ashland Theatre, 130

Ashland Train Days, 130

BBGB Tales for Kids, 133

Beauvine, 27

Belle Isle, 60, 67, 71, 74

Belle Isle Craft Spirits, 21

Belmont Butchery, 124

Bill "Bojangles" Robinson Statue, 89

Bingo Beer Co., 48–49

Black Heath Meadery, 18–19

Black History Museum & Cultural Center of Virginia, 89

Black Rabbit Tattoo, 117

Blandford Church, 92–93

Book Bar, The, 133

Book People, 133

Boulevard Burger & Brews, 27

Brown's Island, 40, 55, 67, 68

Bryant's Cidery & Brewery, 19

Buskey Cider, 18–19

Buttermilk Trail, 74

Bygones Vintage, 118

Byrd Theatre, 34

Caboose Market and Café, 131

Canal Walk, 66–67

Capitol Hill, 96

Capitol Square, 107

Caravati's Architectural Salvage, 128

Carena's Jamaican Grille, 12

Carytown, 110

Carytown Watermelon Festival, 110

Center of the Yarniverse, 131

Chadwick & Son Orchids, 122

Changing Reins, 131

Children's Museum of Richmond, 45

Chimborazo Hospital and Medical Museum, 92–93, 94

Church Hill, 5, 52, 94, 96

Circuit Arcade Bar, 49

Cirrus Vodka, 21

CMoR Chesterfield, 45

Coalition Theater, 36–37

Cobra Burger, 5

ComedySportz, Richmond, 36–37

Court End, 96

Courthouse Creek Cider, 18–19

Cove, The, 74

Crafted, 24

Croaker's Spot, 31

Crossroads Art Center, 120

Discover Richmond Tours, 52
Dominion Energy Center, 44
Dorey Park, 64, 79
DraftCade, 49
Edo's Squid, 29
Elegba Folklore Society, 89
Fan District, 52
Fancy Biscuit, The, 8
Final Gravity Brewing, 16–17
Firehouse Theatre, 50
First Friday Art Walks, 105
Floodwall Park, 66–67
For the Love of Chocolate, 111
Forest Hill Park, 74
Fountain Bookstore, 132
Franklin Street, 96
Friday Cheers, 55
Funktastic Meads, 18–19
George Washington Equestrian
    Monument, 107
Gillie's Creek Park, 78
Godfrey's, 53
Governor's Mansion, 107
Great Shiplock Park, 64
Grisette, 5
GWARbar, 28
Hardywood Park Craft Brewery, 15
Haunts of Richmond, 96
Havana '59, 51
Henricus Historical Park, 102
Henry Box Brown Monument, 66
Henry Clay Inn, 130
Heroes & Ghosts Tattoo, 117
Hill Café, The, 5
Hippodrome Theater, 89
Hollywood Cemetery, 98–99
Hotel Greene, 54

Isley Brewing Company, 15
Jackson Ward, 88, 89, 119
Jamaica House, 12
James River, 23, 71, 73, 86, 94, 98, 102
James River Cellars Winery, 23
James River Park System, 60, 72
James River Steam Brewery beer caves,
    15, 64
Jasper, The, 26, 52
Jefferson, The, 10, 52
Jonesin' for a Treat Dog Treats, 114
Joseph Bryan Park, 79
Kickstand, 65
Kitchen Classroom, 22
Kuba Kuba, 13
Kuba Kuba Dos, 13
Kul Wheels Electric Bikes, 65
L'Opossum, 4
La Milpa Restaurant, 9
LaDiff, 127
Leake's Mill Park, 72
Legend Brewing Company, 15
Lemaire at the Jefferson Hotel, 10
Lewis Ginter Botanical Garden, 85
Lex's of Carytown, 111
Libby Hill Park, 94
Liberty Public House, 5
Light Up the Tracks, 130
Little Bookshop, The, 133
Loose Screw Tattoo, 116
Lumpkin's Jail, 90
Maggie L. Walker National Historic
    Site, 88
Main Street Station, 90, 106
Mama J's, 31
Manchester Climbing Wall, 74
Manchester Docks, at Ancarrow's
    Landing, The, 90

140

Mantle, 107

Maymont, 86

Mekong Restaurant, 14

Mending Walls Project, 100

Metro Richmond Zoo, 46

Metzger Bar & Butchery, 5

Mise En Place, 22

Modlin Center for the Arts at University of Richmond, 56

Mongrel, 126

Monument Avenue 10k, 70

Mother Shrub Drinking Vinegar, 114

National Battlefield Park, Richmond, Headquarters, 92–93

National, The, 35

Nightingale Ice Cream Sandwiches, 114

Nile, The, 5

North Bank Trail, 60

Old Original Bookbinder's Seafood & Steakhouse, 11

Oregon Hill, 74

Pamplin Historical Park & The National Museum of the Civil War Soldier, 93

PARK365, 75

Park, The, 49

Patrick Henry's Pub & Grille, 5

Peak Experiences, 74

Petersburg National Battlefield, Eastern Front Visitor Center, 93

Pipeline Walk, 60, 67

Plan 9 Music, 125

Pocahontas State Park, 62, 72

Poe Museum, The, 87, 96

Pony Pasture, 71, 74

Poor Farm Park, 72

Pop of Confetti, 111

Proper Pie, 5

Pump House, 60

Randolph-Macon College, 130

Reservoir Distillery, 20–21

Richmond Beer Trail, 15

Richmond Flying Squirrels at The Diamond, 61

Richmond Folk Festival, 40, 125

Richmond Funny Bone, 37

Richmond Greek Festival, 2

Richmond International Dragon Boat Festival, 76

Richmond Kickers at City Stadium, 63

Richmond Marathon, Half, and 8k, 70

Richmond Mural Project, 100

Richmond Raceway, 69

Richmond Railroad Museum, 106

Richmond Road Runners Club, 70

Richmond Slave Trail, 90

Richmond Sports Backers, 70

Richmond Symphony, 44, 57

Richmond Tattoo Art & Music Festival, 117

Richmond Triangle Players, 43

Riverside Cycling, 72

Riverside Outfitters, 73

Robins Nature Center, 86

Rocketts Landing, 76, 90

Roosevelt, The, 5

Ruff Canine Club, 77

RVA Big Market, 112

RVA Trail Report, 72

Sally Bell's, 3

Salvation Tattoo Gallery, 117

Science Museum of Virginia, 103, 106

Scott's Addition, 15

Sedona Tap House, 24

Shakoor's Merchandise, 119

Shelf Life Books, 133

Shockoe Bottom, 11, 82, 90, 106, 132

Shops at 5807, The, 121

• •

Shyndigz, 8

Slingshot Social Game Club, 49

Southern Kitchen, 31

Spotty Dog Ice Cream Co., 5

St. John's Church, 94–95

Station 2, 27

Stella's, 2

Stone Brewing, Richmond, 16–17, 78

Strangeways Brewing, 15

Sub Rosa Bakery, 5

Swift Creek Mill Theatre, 43

T. Tyler Potterfield Memorial Bridge, 66–67

Thrill of the Hunt, 131

Tin Pan, The, 38

Tiny Tim's Toys & Trains, 131

Tobacco Company Restaurant, The, 11

Traveling Chic Boutique, 111

Tredegar Iron Works, 92

Triple Crossing Beer, 16–17, 78

Truetimber Disc Golf Course, 79

Ukrop's Market Hall, 6

Uncorked Half and 5k, 70

Upper Shirley Vineyards, 23

Valentine First Freedom Center, The, 82

Valentine Museum and Wickham House, The, 82

Valentine Museum Shop, 114

Väsen Brewing, 16–17

VCUarts, 56

Veil Brewing, The, 17

Virago Spirits, 20–21

Virginia Capital Trail, 23, 64, 79

Virginia Civil Rights Memorial, 107

Virginia Department of Wildlife Resources, 71

Virginia Holocaust Museum, 91

Virginia Museum of Fine Arts, 57, 84

Virginia Museum of History & Culture, 83

Virginia Rep Center for Arts and Education, 42–43

Virginia Repertory Theatre, Barksdale at Hanover Tavern, 42–43

Virginia Repertory Theatre, Sara Belle and Neil November Theatre, 42–43

Virginia Shop at the Library of Virginia, 133

Virginia State Capitol, 107

Virginia War Memorial, 104

Virginia Women's Monument, 107

Visual Arts Center of Richmond, The, 39

White House of the Confederacy, 92–93

World of Mirth, 111

Zombie Walk, 110

ZZQ, 25